Making it as a Teach

Teaching is a delightfully rewarding, wonderfully enlightening and diverse career. Yet, at present, teacher recruitment and retention are in crisis, with some of the most at risk of leaving the profession being those in their early years of teaching. *Making it as a Teacher* offers a variety of tips, anecdotes, real-life examples and practical advice to help new teachers survive and thrive through the first 5 years of teaching, from the first-hand experiences of a teacher and middle leader.

Divided into thematic sections, *Making It, Surviving* and *Thriving*, the book explores the issues and challenges teachers may face, including:

- Lesson planning, marking and feedback

- Behaviour and classroom management

- Work-life balance

- Progression, CPD and networking

With the voices of teaching professionals woven throughout, this is essential reading for new teachers, those undertaking initial teacher training, QT mentors and other teaching staff that support new teachers in the early stages of their career.

Victoria Hewett is Subject Leader for Geography and Environmental Systems and Societies at Tonbridge Grammar School, Tonbridge, UK. Victoria tweets as @MrsHumanities, blogs at www.mrshumanities.com, and has been a UK Blog Award Education Finalist for three years running.

Making it as a Teacher

How to Survive and Thrive in the First Five Years

Victoria Hewett

Routledge
Taylor & Francis Group

LONDON AND NEW YORK

First published 2019
by Routledge
2 Park Square, Milton Park, Abingdon, Oxon OX14 4RN

and by Routledge
52 Vanderbilt Avenue, New York, NY 10017

Routledge is an imprint of the Taylor & Francis Group, an informa business

British Library Cataloguing-in-Publication Data
A catalogue record for this book is available from the British Library

Library of Congress Cataloging-in-Publication Data
Names: Hewett, Victoria, author.
Title: Making it as a teacher : how to survive and thrive in the first five years / Victoria Hewett.
Description: Abingdon, Oxon ; New York, NY : Routledge, 2019. | Includes bibliographical references and index.
Identifiers: LCCN 2019004467 (print) | LCCN 2019013670 (ebook) | ISBN 9780429489341 (Ebk) | ISBN 9781138593589 (hbk) | ISBN 9781138593596 (pbk) | ISBN 9780429489341 (ebook)
Subjects: LCSH: First year teachers. | Teaching—Vocational guidance. | Classroom management.
Classification: LCC LB2844.1.N4 (ebook) | LCC LB2844.1.N4 H48 2019 (print) | DDC 371.102—dc23
LC record available at https://lccn.loc.gov/2019004467

ISBN: 978-1-138-59358-9 (hbk)
ISBN: 978-1-138-59359-6 (pbk)
ISBN: 978-0-429-48934-1 (ebk)

Typeset in Melior
by Apex CoVantage, LLC

MIX
Paper from
responsible sources
FSC
www.fsc.org   FSC® C013056

Printed and bound in Great Britain by
TJ International Ltd, Padstow, Cornwall

To my GCSE group 2016–2018, for reigniting the flame

To Seb, for protecting it

To Lorette, for fuelling it

Contents

Figures

Contributors

Snippets of Insight were kindly provided by:

Adrian Bethune, Teacher and author of 'Wellbeing in the Primary Classroom: A Practical Guide to Teaching Happiness'. Tweets as @AdrianBethune

Andrew Cowley, Deputy Headteacher and author of 'The Wellbeing Toolkit'. Tweets as @andrew_cowley23

Ed Brodhurst, Assistant Headteacher. Tweets as @brodhurst

Gill Rowland, Senior Lecturer at Canterbury Christ Church University. Tweets as @gillrowland1

Jo Morgan, Maths Lead Practitioner, Harris Federation and UK Blog Award Winner 2017. Tweets as @mathsjem

Maria O'Neill, Pastoral leader (ESafety &PSHE); Founder @UKPastoralChat. Tweets as @DaringOptimist

Rebecca Foster, Head of English. Tweets as @TLPMsF

Rufus Johnstone, Lead Coach. Tweets as @rufuswilliam

Sam Collins, Founder of Schoolwell. Tweets at @samschoolstuff

Sarah Larsen, Teacher of Geography. Tweets as @sarahlarsen74

Foreword

The daily lightbulb moments when students finally understand and master a skill. The difference being made to a child or young person's life every single day. Teaching is one of the most important jobs there is; it is one of the most rewarding professions.

And yet despite this, almost a third of new teachers who started jobs in English state schools in 2010 had left the sector five years later. By 2025 there will be three million pupils of secondary school age, but not enough young people are choosing to join the profession themselves.

Our research suggests that those working in education for less than five years are 29% more likely to experience a mental health problem compared to their colleagues. It is a gap that has widened in recent years, alongside an increase in symptoms such as panic attacks, insomnia, tearfulness and difficulty concentrating.

This is why, as a charity, we are passionate about helping every teacher to feel respected, supported and resilient. And it is why I am privileged to write the foreword for this important and timely publication.

Victoria has been an inspirational ambassador for Education Support Partnership over the past two years, since being supported by our counsellors back in 2016. Her courage to share her story has resonated with thousands of teachers who were feeling the same. She will never truly know the impact she has had on the lives of others.

This book is not just powerful because it delivers a first-hand experience. It is deeply rooted in robust research and evidence-based techniques, many of which are the result of Victoria's innovation and creativity, particularly in relation to control over workload.

The crucial message Victoria gets across is that achieving positive wellbeing is not black and white; it is not something that can be accomplished through a single intervention; neither is it a fixed state. It is the result of a range of professional and personal factors, interacting with wider structural pressures.

Victoria makes the abstract concept of wellbeing tangible and highlights the importance of self-care. Achieving positive wellbeing is at the heart of everything we do and the challenges we face. This is why it is so refreshing to see a book that offers teachers applied, well-informed advice that can be put directly into practice.

I predict this book will be the first of many, for someone who is destined to be a leading voice within the sector in the years ahead. We are incredibly fortunate to have her connected to the charity and hugely proud of what she has accomplished through this piece of work.

And a final message to those joining this wonderful profession:

As with any people-centred job, there will be challenges. However, this year we are seeing the sector taking seriously the need for meaningful change, which will deliver improvements as you start out in your career. And remember, if you ever find yourself struggling or sense that you are not at your best, Education Support Partnership exists for YOU – we are only ever a phone call away!

Sinéad Mc Brearty
Acting CEO, Education Support Partnership

Preface

When I set up my blog, Mrs Humanities, I did so because I felt lonely in teaching. I wanted to share ideas, discuss pedagogy and develop my practice. I never at any point expected it would lead to everything it has: articles in magazines and on websites, speaking at conferences and events, being a finalist in the UK blog awards and an invitation to write a book.

These accomplishments seemed even more unlikely when I reached rock bottom in April 2016. At the time I thought I would never return to the classroom. Let alone that I would love teaching again.

I've been very lucky to find a school that makes me feel supported and valued. A school that has given me autonomy and trust. A school that I enjoy working in most days.

Not everyone is so lucky. I want this book to help those that are new to teaching and already thinking that it might not be for them. Those that have qualified but can't continue as they are. Those that are thinking of leaving before they've really cemented their practice. This is for you.

Acknowledgements

I would like to thank my Husband for always, always being there no matter how difficult I got, my Mum and Dad who have always given me support and encouragement even despite the distance between us and Lorette for being my personal cheerleader.

I also need to say thank you to all those that contributed to the book through their snippets of insight and wisdom.

Finally, I'd like to say a big thank you to the Education Support Partnership; without their helpline I may well have left teaching for good. Thank you.

Abbreviations

ACE	Accept, challenge, extend
ADHD	Attention deficit hyperactivity disorder
ASD	Autistic spectrum disorder
CPD	Continued Professional Development
DfE	Department for Education (UK)
DIRT	Directed Improvement and Reflection Time
EYFS	Early Years Foundation Stage
EEF	Education Endowment Foundation
Ebacc	English Baccalaureate
FE	Further education
GCSE	General Certificate of Secondary Education
HoD	Head of Department
HLTA	Higher level teaching assistant
ICT	Information communication technology
ITT	Initial teacher training
INSET	In-service training day
IB	International Baccalaureate
KS1-5	Key Stage
LA	Local Authority
MAT	Multi-academy trust
NUT	National Union of Teachers
NVQ	National Vocational Qualification
NQT	Newly Qualified Teacher
Ofsted	Office for Standards in Education, Children's Services and Skills
PPA	Planning, preparation and assessment
PD	Professional Development
PGCE	Postgraduate certificate in education
PoL	Programme of learning
QTS	Qualified Teaching Status
RQT	Recently Qualified Teacher

RAG	Red, amber and green
SoW	Scheme of Work
SLT	Senior Leadership Team
SEN	Special educational needs
SENCO	Special educational needs Coordinator
SpLN	Specific Learning Needs
SLCN	Speech, Language and Communication Needs
SKE	Subject Knowledge Enhancement
SL	Subject Leader
TLR	Teaching and Learning Responsibility
TA	Teaching assistant
TES	Times Educational Supplement
WABOLL	What a bad one looks like
WAGOLL	What a good one looks like
WCF	Whole-Class Feedback

Introduction

Teaching is hard. Full Stop.

So far in my career as a teacher, I've never met anyone that has gone into teaching truly believing that it's a case of finish at 3:30 pm, no work on weekends and holidays galore. Instead we go into teaching for a variety of reasons, whether it be to make a difference, for the love of our subject or to shape the minds of future generations. Whatever our reasons, each one is influenced by our prior experiences, our circumstance and our outlook on the world.

Yet at present we have a teacher retention issue in the UK, and it's not only that teaching is losing its appeal to newcomers.

A report on teacher retention in 2017 from NFER suggests that between '10–11% of qualified teachers leave each year with 39,000 working age teachers leaving state schools in 2015, compared to 27,910 in 2011' (Dez-Clays, 2017) yet with pupil numbers in secondary schools set to increase by 20% in the next ten years the pressure is on for schools to retain and attract new staff.

The report *Teacher workload and professional development in England's secondary schools: insights from TALIS* (2016) from the Education Policy Institute helps to demonstrate just some of the reasons for the UK's retention and recruitment crisis.

Findings of the Education Policy Institute report using data from Teaching and Learning International Survey (TALIS) in 2016 concluded the following:

- Teachers in the UK are working longer hours than in most other countries.

  - Full-time teachers work on average 48.2 hours per week.

- Long working hours are hindering teachers' access to CPD.

  - Average days spent on CPD in the UK equates to just four days in comparison to an average of 10.5 in other countries.

■ UK teachers at risk of 'burn out', especially in the early stages of careers.

- Starting pay for teachers in England is 16% lower than the OECD average.
- Only 48% of teachers in England have more than ten years' experience, compared to an average of 64% in other OECD countries.

Yet some of those most at risk of leaving the profession are those in their early years of teaching: those that are passionate and needed to maintain the teaching profession in the future. From my experience, I completely understand why many of those leaving are new teachers that have yet to make it through the first five years of their teaching career. In fact in October 2016, Nick Gibb stated that 'of the 21,400 who began teaching in English state schools in 2010, 30% had quit by 2015'. But why?

To start with it's the long hours, the Department for Education's '*Teacher Workload Survey 2016*' published February 2017, indicated that teachers in their first six years of teaching work a greater number of hours than their experienced counterparts, with the average weekly hours worked at primary being 59.5 and at secondary being 55.2 (Higton et al., 2017).

Then there's the scrutiny and performance management which puts huge amounts of pressure on both early-career teachers and the more experienced. Teaching is challenging enough with the variety of roles, tasks and paperwork we're expected to do outside of the day-to-day delivery of lessons; add to that the pressure of always being watched, judged and scrutinised, and you're creating a stress bomb just waiting to explode.

Teaching is really hard at times, but it's also incredibly fulfilling. I might be starting to sound like one of the 'Get into Teaching' adverts now, but it really is. Every day is different. Students bring a light into your life that helps to keep you young at heart; they inspire you and motivate you (even the more challenging ones that cause you a mountain of work, but that have a great amount of potential). Teaching truly is brilliant.

As you'll soon read, I didn't do a PGCE to become a full-time teacher, but I fell in love with the classroom and couldn't imagine doing anything else after that. It hasn't been smooth sailing at all, but I've been determined and resilient enough to make it through the other side. And, well, now I'm writing a book on it. I don't claim to be an expert in a lot of what I discuss, just a practitioner that has researched and tried a lot of strategies to find what works for me and my context.

The following will give you some insight into my journey toward becoming the teacher I am today. I share it because I reached rock bottom within the first five years: a breakdown, depression and desperation to leave, but I've also recovered from it, made changes and feel I am currently thriving. Throughout my time in teaching I've implemented many strategies, some I've refined, some I've ditched, but all have influenced my day-to-day practice and helped me to become a better, happier teacher.

Within 'Making it as Teacher' I draw upon my own experiences to provide you with insight and possible solutions to overcoming your own potential problems to help you to survive and thrive in teaching.

Becoming a teacher: my story

Teaching. It was on my list of aspirations growing up. My mum worked in a school first as a cleaner, then as a dinner lady, and now she's a been a TA at the school for fourteen years. I'd meet her after school; I'd talk to the teachers; I'd spend time in the classrooms; I'd enjoy the environment I found myself in.

At the age of 15 I undertook work experience at my mum's school. I loved it, but I was also given a realistic insight to the hours worked and the paperwork expected. After that I decided I'd focus on geography rather than teaching. I went to sixth form college and university all with the aim of working in coastal management.

It was only when I found myself working at the Centre for Alternative Energy that my mind changed. I loved educating people about environmental issues, the possibilities and the solutions to global problems. I loved working with the public and in particular, young people. My mind was influenced when I was working with a school group from Birmingham. On arrival one of the students was incredibly excited; he exclaimed "I've just seen a real-life cow, it was even in a McDonald's cheeseburger". That moment ignited a new aspiration into Environmental Education. I'd get to work in the subject I enjoy whilst also working in the area I'd aspired to throughout my childhood – education.

From there I took an Internship at Global Action Plan which developed my love for and experience of environmental education. After that I applied for a PGCE, with the sole aim that it would make my applications for environmental education jobs more desirable as these positions were few and far between.

When I went into teaching, I never expected to stay. My plan was to work a year or two to gain experience and then start looking for opportunities in the environmental sector.

What I hadn't anticipated though, is that I would stay in teaching; that I would enjoy the experience of leading a classroom as much as I did. Teaching has become a major part of my life, and despite the several occasions where I've tried or wanted to walk away, I'm extremely proud to be a teacher.

Reaching this point hasn't been an easy journey, but it has been an adventure with numerous ups and downs. I've learnt a great deal about pedagogy, about people and about myself as a result of both smooth and turbulent times.

ITT

I started my career by undertaking a PGCE at Aberystwyth University in 2010–2011. My partner and I struggled financially as he was unable to secure a job once we moved to Mid-Wales. He ended up moving back to Kent to live with family whilst I finished the course. The placement schools were both over 30 miles away, and since I didn't drive, I relied on public transport. This alone exhausted me.

I loved my first placement; I left feeling confident and positive about my abilities. My second placement wasn't as commendable. My confidence plummeted, and my emotions ran high; I constantly questioned my ability to teach and felt unsupported by my mentor. My mentor didn't approve of many of my approaches and took enmity towards my introverted nature. By April 2011, I was on the verge of dropping out of my PGCE when my university mentor raised my confidence and demonstrated her faith in me. I made it through the remainder of the year and passed the PGCE with QTS in geography and ICT.

Despite the struggles, by the end of the course I was eager to continue to teach. I wanted to stay in the classroom. I hadn't anticipated how much I would enjoy it. Environmental education was no longer on my career radar. I wanted to be a TEACHER.

Despite passing and loving teaching, my confidence was at an all-time low, and the prospect of applying to schools filled me with dread. I applied to a select few in the southeast near where my partner's family were located. But by the end of the summer I still hadn't secured a position. I therefore took the difficult decision to work outside of classroom teaching to earn enough money to put down a rental deposit. I secured a job in an EYFS setting where I worked for eight months.

Working in early years gave me my confidence back. The other staff frequently endorsed my ideas and approaches, and before I knew it I was being asked to undertake an NVQ in child care and development in an attempt to propel me into a management position. I had to decline though; working with the 3–5 year olds made me thirsty for the classroom. I wanted to get back in front of students and share my love of geography. I started to apply for jobs and very quickly accepted a position at a school some 30 miles away. I was thrilled but also sad to say goodbye to the early years.

Year I

My NQT year was interesting. I worked with some amazing educators and a fantastic department. The school was tough with high expectations for staff and often challenging students, but I always felt incredibly supported by my department and NQT coordinator.

During this time, I lived 30 miles from work. Although the journey wasn't too arduous, I didn't drive. I never needed to learn living in Cardiff and Aberystwyth, where public transport was reliable and cheap. Luckily a wonderful woman came to my rescue, she lived in the same town and was also an NQT. She was older than me and had entered the profession after gaining a wealth of experience elsewhere; dare I say it, she became like a mother to me with all her words of advice and constant reminders of work/life balance. Even when I eventually passed my driving test, we continued to car share.

Just as we settled into the new school year, the week before the October half term we had the call from Ofsted. I'd been teaching for just seven weeks and was observed. To say I was nervous would be an understatement. I was observed with a tricky high-ability year 8 group; I had really hoped I wouldn't be observed that lesson. The feedback was very positive though: good with outstanding features. I couldn't complain.

After the stress of Ofsted at the beginning I didn't think it could get much worse. Oh, how I was wrong. I never realised how much work would be involved with behaviour, let alone with planning, marking and assessment. The school was a challenging one. The staff were great, supportive and incredibly helpful; but SLT expectations were high, and behaviour was a major battle at times.

It was long hours. I'd find myself having to phone home to parents and carers most nights of the week after a long and challenging day teaching. This would then be followed by several hours of marking books. I'd ensure I was prepared for lessons over the weekend, spending the entirety of Sunday planning and often part of Saturday.

The holidays consisted of little rest and mostly marking. The end of every half term, Key Stage 3 classes would sit a test. These tests had to be marked over the holidays so that data could be inputted the first week back. Books had to be marked every four lessons with positives and targets. In just a one-week half-term holiday I recall having ninety books, thirty controlled assessments plus tests for every Key Stage 3 class that I taught at the time to assess and mark.

This was the norm to me. I didn't know any different. Many of the teachers were either new and in the same boat or experienced thus well-resourced and respected by students. I know some of you will be reading this and thinking this could be describing your circumstances at present.

Year 2

I stayed at the same school and felt confident that this year would be better. I knew the routines, more of the students, the GCSE courses etc. It should have been a breeze, and to start with, it was until my projector broke in the first term. Oh dear!

Having no projector meant that all my resources from the year before were somewhat redundant. Additionally, since the photocopying budget was low, printing was restricted. This meant that teaching lessons suddenly became a lot more difficult. Unfortunately, it was going to be several weeks for the parts to be delivered because I just so happened to have an 'old' projector.

This experience taught me how to teach without technology and resources. I relied on my knowledge and the whiteboard. I used models that students had made the previous year to demonstrate, for instance, rainforest structure; I became more imaginative in my approach. But it was very hard work.

The tip of the iceberg came just after I'd been told to relax on my marking by the Headteacher. He recognised how hard I was working and that my marking was top of the school, but I was working myself into the ground. Yet we had a Mocksted, and the external observer gave me terrible feedback. Firstly, they commented that I hadn't shared the learning objectives with students. The contrary was true: they were written on the whiteboard and at the top of the student instruction sheets, and if they'd been there at the start of the lesson they would have heard me read and discuss them with the class. They commented on my poor planning, yet there were a range of activities with plenty of differentiation to suit individual needs and to challenge my more able students. Finally, the negative comment on my marking. . . . MY MARKING! "Insufficient!" I blew my top at that. My Head of Department was not happy, the Headteacher certainly didn't agree and essentially the whole observation was wiped off the record. The school threw a big party that Christmas . . . many of us felt it was a way to say sorry for the terrible Mocksted experience, especially as we'd received an Outstanding the year before from the official Ofsted.

After that experience, by the time half term came I was exhausted and didn't feel I wanted to go back to school. I'd fallen into a state of depression, which I hadn't realised at the time, but looking back that's exactly what it was. I started experiencing dizziness and vertigo as well which almost led me to passing out in front of a class, and which led to several visits to the GP and hospital.

The school provided some counselling which helped, and I eventually applied for Head of Humanities at a different school, closer to home. I managed to get the position in February 2014 and handed in my notice to end at Easter. Whilst the Head did not seem happy with my decision, I'm sure deep down he recognised that it was the best thing for me at the time.

The school I was joining should have been my forever school: a land-based school with sustainability at its heart. When the school was first announced as I undertook my PGCE, I knew I wanted to work there and that I would one day. Unfortunately, my dream school turned out to be my nightmare. I won't go into too many details, but the relentless workload, lack of support to maintain staff wellbeing and the overwhelming stress became too much, and I eventually had a breakdown. I'll tell you more about that later.

The first term there was different. I taught Humanities as well as art, drama and cookery. I was out of my comfort zone with the last three but survived until the summer.

Year 3

Year 3 went by in a whirlwind. Being a new school, there was a hell of a lot of work involved in setting up whole and departmental resources and routines. We were a small community, and it felt like that to begin with. Everyone was supportive of one another; we ate together and chatted when we could.

As a consistent team of staff emerged, the kids became better behaved, and the consistency helped many of them to feel better about school. In fact, what became more challenging was the workload. Being a new school, we had regular visits from a DfE representative (I think) who would observe the progress of the school, staff and students. We'd have one per term, along with other observations as part of the self-evaluation weeks. For each observation we had to provide data packs on classes, flightpaths on books, targets and progress on the front covers etc. The amount of paper being used was huge, and that was before we thought about resourcing lessons and scaffolding for students.

Anyway, I did what I had to do and got through. There were times when I wanted to just give up, but I kept on thanks to the support of my family and closest colleagues. By June we had Ofsted and it was a very positive experience. I felt confident, and it came across; the inspector had no feedback on how I could improve. Brilliant. My marking and feedback was also highly recognised and praised by the inspection team.

My feedback, not marking, approach was beginning to take shape, and as result I ended up running a CPD session in the final term for current and new staff on marking and feedback strategies.

Whilst it had been a difficult year in terms of workload, #Teacher5aday and Twitter had helped me through the rollercoaster, and I finished the school year on a relative high (although I was disappointed that we didn't celebrate our excellent Ofsted result).

Year 4

This was the year of my undoing. This was the year I came closest to walking out of teaching once and for all. This was the year when it all became too much. The workload, the behaviour, the level of SEN, the lack of support, the lack of specific CPD . . . the staff morale. In fact, I think staff morale had the biggest impact. Seeing people working as hard as they were and receiving no or little recognition and appreciation for it. Instead it seemed we were just having more and more work piled onto us.

If the workload wasn't relentless enough, I felt unsupported by SLT. Behaviour was worsening and despite following the school procedures, kids seemed to be getting away with the highest of sanctions. I'd always follow through at my end, but sanctions weren't exactly followed through at the top. This made teaching harder and harder.

I started looking and writing applications for jobs outside of teaching, but I was too scared to send them. I wouldn't be able to finish until the summer; would they even wait that long? I wrote many but didn't send any.

Then the penultimate day before the Easter break I eventually broke down in front of a class. The poor handful of students that wanted to learn in this class – their enthusiasm for learning had slowly declined; their patience for others dwindled. I hated seeing this and burst into tears in front of the class, and between sobs I ranted about how much I wanted them to achieve and do well, but that chosen behaviours were holding them and their peers back. By the end of the lesson, I felt embarrassed and ashamed for my emotional outburst.

I tried to enjoy the Easter half break but instead I ended up working most of it, marking assessments and planning for the next term. When I returned to school, I couldn't do it.

I walked into my classroom and walked right back out again. The anxiety was too much. I walked away. I made my way inside the main building a member of staff caught me, asked if I was okay. That was it, their concern set me off and tears just streamed. I sat in the meeting room for what felt like hours sobbing. I eventually went home, not that I remember how I got there. The rest of the day is a complete blur.

I couldn't return the next day or the next and eventually I was signed off. Three weeks I spent away from the classroom, and although it helped I still didn't feel ready to head back.

During my time off, I'd received notification that I'd been offered an interview for a job I'd applied for. I went to the interview and whilst I liked the school and they liked me, I felt I needed time to process the offer. In the interview, I'd asked about staff wellbeing and this essentially confirmed to me that it would be a good school to work at. After speaking to my current Headteacher, I decided that accepting the offer was most certainly the best thing to do.

My return to school was hard. I wasn't ready, but I was pressured into returning – I won't go into the details. I returned and the kids were amazing. They were happy to see me, and even those that had been difficult before Easter had somewhat improved. I didn't share why I'd been off, but the kids made up a wonderful story about fighting crocodiles in some far off tropical land and being injured and so on. It was a relief when they just made a light-hearted joke of my time away.

I struggled through the remainder of the year and left feeling loved by the students. The array of gifts and messages were heart-warming. It's not until you leave that you realise how appreciated you are. I do miss many of the kids; I'd formed some fantastic bonds with some of my classes, and it was hard to say goodbye to them. But if I hadn't accepted the job after support from the Education Support Network, I know I would have ended up leaving the school and teaching.

Year 5 and onwards

This stage has been my journey from breakdown to recovery. I've seen my career and happiness flourish. It has reignited my fire for teaching and helped me to open the door on mental health in teaching. I'm glad I stayed in teaching and tried one more school. I can see this as my forever school.

There have been a few ups and downs, a struggle here and there but on the whole, it was nothing compared to my prior experiences. Nothing I couldn't handle with a bit of determination and dare I say it . . . resilience.

In my first year at the school, the number of times that reducing workload and staff wellbeing was discussed in meetings blew me away; to have a senior leadership team that cared so much about its staff and students really meant a lot to me. I feel appreciated and respected as an educator and member of staff. I wish every school could make their staff feel this way.

I hope that by reading my story it helps you to understand where my experiences lie and why I'm writing this book to support teachers, particularly those new to the profession, in finding happiness and a work-life balance.

Going forward

So why read this book?

Whilst the education system and teaching profession needs top-down support from Government, Ofsted and other influential institutions, we also need to create change from the bottom-up by taking action for ourselves; in doing so we challenge workload, improve our wellbeing and stand up for our profession. This book aims to help you do that, to take charge, to remain in the classroom and to thrive whilst you're at it.

My hope is that this book supports you, the new (and maybe even experienced) teachers in understanding the challenges you may face, to support you in finding solutions to problems you may currently be in or might encounter and to enable you to recognise that you are not alone in any of the more negative experiences you may come across. But I also want to provide you with hope, hope that you can love teaching as much as you might want, that you can manage your workload and improve your wellbeing without leaving this brilliant profession.

The book has been divided into three sections to achieve this: 'Making It', 'Surviving' and 'Thriving'. You'll be taken on a journey from entering the profession to becoming a flourishing part of it. Moving you from surviving to thriving in teaching.

In 'Making It' we will explore what it means to be a teacher both professionally and personally, the challenges of the teaching profession and why despite those challenges, education is an extraordinarily inspiring, rewarding and diverse profession to be a part of.

In 'Surviving' we will look at what we can do for ourselves to ease the workload and associated stresses. In this section we will explore how we can set up our classrooms to work for us, ideas and strategies to simplify lesson planning, differentiation and marking along with suggestions to develop effective classroom management in the early years of teaching. We end this section by exploring wellbeing and burnout with strategies to avoid it by helping you to take charge of your own wellbeing.

Before concluding, we will explore ways to help teachers not just survive but truly thrive in the profession. Teaching shouldn't just be a case of surviving each day, term or academic year. To help you to thrive this section explores ways to develop your subject knowledge and professional practice cheaply, without large time commitments through CPD and networking. We will also explore and consider taking on responsibility within the first five years, the potential problems and benefits for new teachers with insight from those that have.

Within the sections we will take a look at a variety of challenges associated with being a teacher such as lesson planning, marking and behaviour and explore strategies for overcoming issues you may face. You will find ideas and tips to help implement a 'less is more' approach to your practice to support your wellbeing and workload making this book as much about self-care as it is teaching and learning.

Many chapters are supported with snippets of insight from Teachers and Education Professionals across the UK from a range of backgrounds including primary, secondary and ITT, giving insight into the range of perspectives and experiences. Throughout you will find personal anecdotes and tales from my experiences to provide a view into the highs, the lows and the solutions in the hope that it will give you hope when times are difficult.

So, as you read this book, try things out and reflect. Find what works for you and scrap those that don't. Discuss with other teachers and reach out if you need to. Most importantly, find your love for teaching.

References

Dez-Clays, Z. (2017) *Teacher retention: Are England's teachers leaving?* [pdf] National Foundation for Educational Research. Available at www.nfer.ac.uk/publications/FFEE05/FFEE05.pdf [Accessed 3rd March 2018]

Gibb, N. (2016) *Teachers: Labour turnover: Written question – 47083* [Online] Available at www.parliament.uk/business/publications/written-questions-answers-statements/written-question/Commons/2016-10-07/47083/ [Accessed 3rd March 2018]

Higton, J. et al. (2017) *Teacher workload survey 2016 research report February 2017* [pdf] Department for Education. Available at www.isc.co.uk/media/4410/tws_2016_final_research_report_feb_2017.pdf [Accessed 3rd March 2018]

Sellen, P. (2016) *Teacher workload and professional development in England's secondary schools: Insights from TALIS* [pdf] Education Policy Institute. Available at https://epi.org.uk/wp-content/uploads/2018/01/TeacherWorkload_EPI.pdf [Accessed 3rd March 2018]

Making it

We all take a different route on our journey to becoming the teachers we are or want to be. For some making it as a teacher can be a smooth ride, whilst for others it's far bumpier ride.

For some of us, the experiences we go through during our training, NQT induction or initial years can make us doubt and question whether being a teacher is the right career for us; to debate whether we should continue this journey and to contemplate if we really want to make it as a teacher.

For those that reach this point, some will simply need a reminder of what it means to be a teacher, whilst others may need to find an alternative to their current situation.

Throughout this section we will explore what it means to be a teacher both in the professional and personal sense to act as a reminder for those less than satisfactory days. You will find top tips and advice on how to make the Teacher Standards work for you during your ITT and NQT induction and insight into the many challenges of the career. Insight of that serves to merely highlight current and potential troubles new teachers may experience as they enter the profession. We finish by exploring possible solutions to help new teachers to stay in the profession, supported with plenty of insight from those that have made changes, made it as a teacher and are now thriving in the profession that they love.

What it means to be a teacher

Let me start with a seemingly simple question.

What is a teacher?

You may be thinking that there's a quite straightforward answer to that – something along the lines of a teacher is somebody that teaches, inspires and enables students to learn. But is that all?

A teacher plans lessons, learning and progress. A teacher supports, enables and facilities learning. A teacher also marks, assesses and reports progress. A teacher analyses and manages data. A teacher provides safety, consistency and opportunities. A teacher listens, guides and supports. A teacher acts as a mentor, counsellor and leader. Being a teacher is so much more than just the teaching.

Simply put the role of a teacher is extremely diverse.

Opportunity to think

What do you see as being fundamental to what it means to be a 'teacher'?

When I think back to my school days I often wonder what made my teachers stay in the classroom. It couldn't have been easy for them teaching in such a deprived area. I remember an occasion when a student in my class brought in a ball bearing gun and was shooting it at teachers and students alike, the day when a fellow student hit a teacher after having dived across the classroom at her; I remember the torment new teachers would receive especially those teaching religious education. My peers were awful at times. Yet when I returned to undertake a two-week placement before embarking on my PGCE seven years later, I returned only to see a large swathe of the same teachers sitting in the staff room. It made me wonder: what kept them there?

Why do people choose to stay in a job that is so challenging at times? What makes us want to be in those classrooms, those school corridors, those school offices? Far more important than the what or how of teaching is the why; why teach?

Opportunity to think

Take a moment to really consider your answer to this question: Why teach?
Was it . . .
To make a difference? In what ways would you envisage this difference?
To enthuse minds to love your subject? Why? What's the importance of your subject?
To inspire change? What kind of change would you expect to see?
Perhaps take a moment to write these thoughts and ideas down to review and reflect
   on during those challenging moments.

As a teacher you will have good days; you'll have bad days. Days that are overwhelming and tiring and days that leave you feeling awesome and euphoric. Days that make you believe you are the best teacher in the world, but also days that will leave you feeling like the worst. No matter how challenging the job becomes at times, it's important to always remember the why. Why do you teach?

Remembering the why

- Draw up a list of all the things you love about teaching for regular review and reflection.

- Write your 'why' on a postcard and keep it on your desk or wall as a reminder.

- Note down and keep messages of gratitude from students.

- Keep a positivity box or journal and record happy moments from your classroom and school day.

- Create a positive mantra for yourself, for those days when you feel you just can't do it anymore.

Teaching is an incredible career, it is hard, challenging and exhausting, but when you see students' progress, dream big and achieve, it makes every moment of negativity worth it. Just remember your why.

Snippets of insight

Each and every one of us will give different reasons for joining the profession. For some it will have been their lifelong aspiration; others may have only considered teaching as they came to the end of their degree. We all have different reasons, but ultimately it is the students we teach that become the focus of our why.

I posed the question "What does it mean to be a teacher?" to some Twitter friends from across the spectrum of positions and different contexts for their insight. Each statement gives vision into our role, our values and our strengths as a profession.

"It means you get to help positively impact and influence the next generation and that they undoubtedly shape and influence you too. It means every day you go into school is a day full of huge potential. Being a teacher means your working life is full of meaning so long as you keep your purpose for being in the classroom at the forefront of your attention". *Adrian Bethune, Teacher and author of 'Wellbeing in the Primary Classroom – A Practical Guide to Teaching Happiness'. Tweets as @AdrianBethune*

"It means having a set of values about the importance of education, about how to model and build positive relationships with young people & learners, about how to value and encourage all learners. It means we keep trying and that we never stop learning ourselves. It also means we build and value relationships with colleagues, parents and all other stakeholders for the best interests of our pupils". *Gill Rowland, Senior Lecturer at Canterbury Christ Church University. Tweets as @gillrowland1*

"Being a teacher means having a really emotionally and intellectually challenging career where you get the wonderful opportunity to share your passion for your favourite subject with the next generation". *Jo Morgan, Maths Lead Practitioner, Harris Federation and UK Blog Award Winner 2017. Tweets as @mathsjem*

"Being a teacher means allowing the children to grow in their values, in the appreciation of their environment and of each other. It means having a love for culture in its many forms and a love of life. Get this right and the students love of learning and having high expectations of themselves will follow". *Andrew Cowley, Deputy Headteacher and author of 'The Wellbeing Toolkit'. Tweets as @andrew_cowley23*

"The meaning of being a teacher is that all your students learn what you want them to learn. That's it. All the beautiful aspects of education funnel through this. It's a straightforward goal that is extremely complex to achieve". *Rufus Johnstone, Lead Coach. Tweets as @rufuswilliam*

"It means being human; being able to establish rapport with colleagues, parents and children. It means that you will never stop learning professionally or personally, and that you will handle whatever the day brings, all whilst you continue to make children fall in love with your subject". *Maria O'Neill, Pastoral leader (ESafety &PSHE); Founder @UKPastoralChat. Tweets as @DaringOptimist*

Takeaways

- Keep a written account of why you want to teach, whether it be a list, a quote or a message on a postcard. Put it somewhere accessible for those challenging days when you need a reminder.

- Keep messages, cards, etc. you receive from students over the time. Take a look at them and remind yourself of the positive impact you've had if and when you're struggling to remember why you bother.

- We all have different reasons for becoming a teacher and different interpretations of what it means to be one, but at the end of the day, we all put our students first in our why. Remember them, even on the days when a student's choices have resulted in your negative mood, they are still growing and learning. Show them compassion but also that choices have consequences.

2 Meeting the standards

Teachers in the UK are expected to work within a set of eight government-specified standards that provide the minimum level of professional practice and conduct expected of qualified teachers.

The standards are initially used to assess those in initial teacher training (ITT) in order to award qualified teaching status (QTS). They also create the backbone of job profiles, performance management and day-to-day teaching once qualified. At times they are used to assess the performance of teachers under scrutiny within capability measures.

As an NQT mentor I recognise the importance of the teachers' standards as a guide for both new and more experienced teachers, but in my experience far too often they are used as a tool for accountability, rather than to support professional development and growth.

The teaching standards shouldn't be something you worry about, instead they should guide and support your practice. In the UK, ITT students and NQTs are expected to demonstrate how they are meeting the standards and the impact of their actions, whilst later on as you progress through the years and become more experienced, the importance of these standards changes. They become the backbone of day-to-day teaching; they influence and guide performance management targets; and they become more of a guide for great teaching and learning.

How to make the teachers' standards work for you

During the ITT year and as NQTs it can be difficult to find the time to reflect and collate how the standards are being met. To make it easier, Bethan White, who I mentored as an NQT, and I worked together to simplify this process over the course of the academic year 2017–2018. We wanted to ensure that the impact folder wouldn't be a massive burden and instead would support Bethan in striving for excellence in her practice.

Together Bethan and I have come up with our top tips to help new teachers to reduce the workload associated with evidencing the standards during the training and the NQT induction process.

- **Create a digital portfolio** – Most ITT courses and NQT induction programmes allow the production of a digital portfolio. We cannot recommend this highly enough. It makes it much easier to collate evidence and cross reference it to the eight teachers' standards. Keep folders for each standard and within them folders for the sub-standards. Put any relevant evidence into the folders such as photos, scanned work and feedback forms. If you feel they apply elsewhere you can simply copy and paste the document or create shortcut. If you're required to document where you are meeting standards, you can also hyperlink to the evidence in your portfolio.

- **Use a QTS Standard Tracker** – Create or download a standard tracker to monitor the provision of evidence for each of the Teachers' Standards. Bethan created a simple excel sheet with each standard. As she provided evidence she RAG rated the table to show her progress in evidencing each core and sub-standard.

- **Create templates** – If the ITT provider or NQT induction programme doesn't provide a template or provides a complex template then create your own (providing this is acceptable). Keep it simple and easy to edit.

- **Think target-process-reflect** – When you've set a target, carefully consider the actions to take place and the process of applying those actions. Afterwards reflect on the impact of process of actions taken: Did you achieve what you set out to achieve? What could have been changed or amended to increase the success rate? Bethan produced several documents that demonstrate her application and reflection effectively without being a time burden.

- **Highlight your planning** – Create a colour-coded key with each of the standards. In your lesson plans, highlight the content that meets any of the standards in the corresponding colour. At the end of the lesson, add a sticky note to your plan and write a short reflective comment or two on the impact of your actions. Simply scan or photograph these to add to your digital portfolio.

- **Keep a reflective journal** – Create a simple template that allows you to reflect on the successes and areas for improvement after each week before setting yourself personal targets to focus on. This helped Bethan to focus on what she wanted to improve in her practice the following week or over the term.

You can download our templates at www.mrshumanities.com/qtstemplates/.

TS1: Set high expectations which inspire, motivate and challenge pupils.

TS1.2: Set goals that stretch and challenge pupils of all backgrounds, abilities and dispositions

In the first term, the year 8 students have been studying the Renaissance. As part of this learning, they must all complete an independent research project on an invention of Leonardo da Vinci. For this project, they should compile a bibliography of Leonardo da Vinci [which we started together in class; a summary of what the invention is (features, characteristics, purpose etc.)]; analyse the strengths and weaknesses of their chosen invention; and finally, compile a bibliography of their research and assess the usefulness and reliability of their sources.

I completed a separate feedback slip per student which assessed them on the 'B' and 'D' criteria for the MYP. Each student was given a mark out of 8 for B and D and then a mark out of 4 for their presentation.

I gave each student a comment for each mark and then individual targets (see below). Instead of writing each target out individually, I created a numbered system so that students had to read carefully through the required list and then write it in their book.

The most common target that was set was one on source analysis; students needed to analyse the sources for their reliability and usefulness.

Targets

1. I need to include precise evidence.
2. I need to explain my points further.
3. I need to create links between my paragraphs.
4. I need to develop my conclusion.
5. I need to use a wider range of sources (books and websites).
6. I need to evaluate my sources to include date, origin, purpose, completeness, intended audience, clarity, comparability, value.
7. I need to improve SPAG (Spelling, punctuation and Grammar).
8. I need to include better diagrams that illustrate my work.
9. I need to improve my bibliography by including:
   For books: Author, Title, date
   For websites: Weblink, date accessed.
10. I need to evaluate the usefulness of my sources.
11. I need to use historical language.

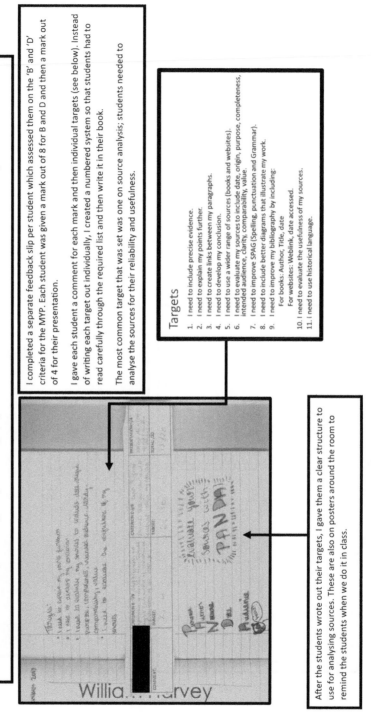

After the students wrote out their targets, I gave them a clear structure to use for analysing sources. These are also on posters around the room to remind the students when we do it in class.

Figure 2.1 Example of the implementation of targets set and reflection on successes and impact

TS1: Set high expectations which inspire, motivate and challenge pupils.

TS1.2: Set goals that stretch and challenge pupils of all backgrounds, abilities and dispositions

In the second half of my feedback lesson, I created an activity that would develop students' source skills so that they could all work towards their target of source analysis.

I created four questions to structure the type of analysis that students would have to do for a 'how useful' question. Students worked in their pairs to answer these questions, whilst also using the PANDA analysis to further analyse. Below is an example of a student's analysis.

1) Study the source below. How useful is the source for explaining the impact of Leonardo da Vinci on the Renaissance?

Source 1: Art historian Bernard Berenson wrote in 1896:
"Leonardo is the one artist of whom it may be said with perfect literalness: Nothing that he touched but turned into a thing of eternal beauty. Whether it be the cross section of a skull, the structure of a weed, or a study of muscles, he, with his feeling for line and for light and shade, forever transmuted it into life-communicating values."

1. When was this source written/made?

4. Your judgement (remember to use the wording of the question!)

2. What evidence can you pick out from this source to answer this question?

3. What does the source not tell you? How can you use your own knowledge?

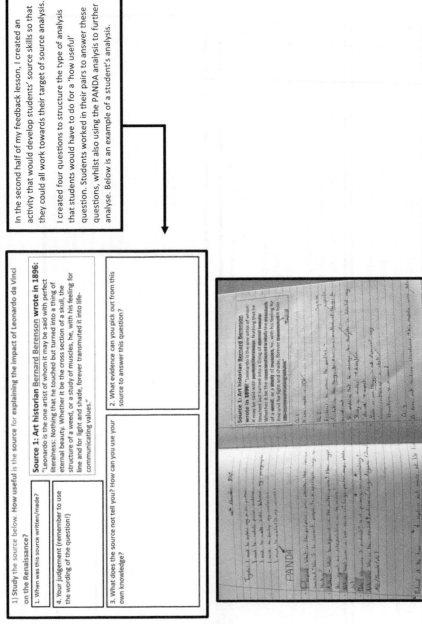

Figure 2.2 Example of the implementation of targets set and reflection on successes and impact

TS1: Set high expectations which inspire, motivate and challenge pupils.

TS1.2: Set goals that stretch and challenge pupils of all backgrounds, abilities and dispositions.

MARCH 2018

Since the last piece of evidence, students have also completed a research project on the British Empire in India. Students were provided with a source pack and had to choose questions from a list to present their information. The students had clear instructions for how to complete this over three lessons and a homework.

How were people treated under the British Empire? An Indian case study.

Task: Fold your A3 page into a booklet.

- Write the title at the top.
- Make sure you have a keywords section with the meaning of each word, this section must include words you think are important from the fact sheet; for example: Raj, Sepoys, Colonialism.

For example: Colonialism: when a country takes political control of another country, occupying it with settlers, and exploiting it economically.

- You must then answer the questions on your question sheet in your booklet.
- Only when all of the questions are answered and your keywords section is finished can you decorate your booklet.

What makes a good information booklet. . .

- Make sure you have clear headings.
- Explain clearly using evidence to back up your answers.
- There are sentence starters to help you if you would like to use them.
- Only decorate your booklet once all of the questions have been answered.
- Don't just copy – you also need to *explain!*
- You MUST complete *AT LEAST five* questions by the end of this lesson.
- You DO NOT have to answer the questions in order.

Students were graded on the variety of sources they used (B), their clear communication and fulfilment of the success criteria (C) and the quality of their Critical Thinking (D). Please see below for some examples of targets set, differentiated according to grades given.

Figure 2.3 Example of the implementation of targets set and reflection on successes and impact

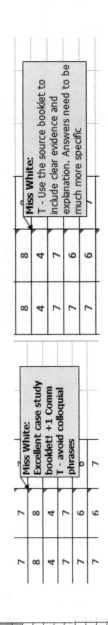

Figure 2.3 (continued)

Date	WWW	EBI	Self-set targets
Monday 4 September 2017	• Met FORM this week. • Dealt with issue of students broken foot: placed her close-by to assess difficulties. • Created PP for the new Y7s that summarised the rules, expectations, timetable, HW etc. They seemed to respond well to this and find it helpful. • School photos, assemblies and briefing. I feel that I am starting to get my head around the timetable more. • I was really pleased with my first Y9 lesson on 'Revolutions' alongside the MYP Enquiry theme. I had the students lead the questioning and the structure for this new topic and we started to discuss different skills we may encounter.	Planning in advance! Due to the quick start to the term, I did not feel fully prepared for lessons long term. Need to create a better overview of the courses.	Keep asking questions if you are not sure. . . Talk with subject leader re Y12 SL assessments
Monday 11 Sept	• Met with prefects for the first time who will help with form time. We have decided what we will be doing for the next few weeks in form time on Mondays. We discussed them supporting the form members in their presentations on alternate weeks. • Historical skills lessons with Y7: The first lesson's timings did not quite work, with too much time spent on the glossary and so the chronology snake ran into the next lesson. For the other two classes, I adapted the lesson so they went off to collect the glossary words sooner and then used peer-support to fill the gaps.	Y10 too much writing. How to combat this? ◊ Worksheets? More discussion? Need to create strategies to be more time efficient, especially in PPAs.	Discuss Y10 with subject team strategies for Y10 and diversifying activities. What is the most time efficient and supportive AND stretching way to do this?

Figure 2.4 Example of NQT reflective journal

Date	WWW	EBI	Self-set targets
Mon 18 Sept	• I have really enjoyed starting to teach the Tollund Man topic. I feel that this has clarified what it means to be a self-led learner/ enquirer for the MYP for me. The first lesson was entirely student led and I found this quite refreshing. • I have then been able to build questioning and start to retain knowledge and better strategies or phrasing of questions across subsequent classes. • Y12 created a keyword list that they had to complete for homework. I created this because many students were not using the correct historical language. This should help them be more specific in the upcoming assessment. WED 20th: First assessed lesson with Subject Leader "Why did the French Revolt?" ◊	Feedback from Subject Leader observation Y9: • Challenge: you should aim to stretch the students further. • Student choices: give students the chance to choose task; this takes a little thought but, once you know the students better, you can guide each one to the most appropriate & challenging task for her. • Make sure that you have additional, extension work for those who finish quickly, or have a look at what they have done and suggest areas for immediate improvement. • Be prepared to discuss: offer the chance for them to put forward and justify their views on an open question. • Get the students to do more of the brain work! • Could start with your homework question and ask the students what questions they would ask to access an answer to it ◊ focuses their research, and question the sources, with the end goal in mind. Your plenary would then have been a discussion of their findings, their justification of their views and so prepare them for the homework.	Talk with NQT mentor about stretch and challenge activities.

Figure 2.4 (Continued)

Your NQT year

Once you're through the training process, you're onto the year of being a Newly Qualified Teacher.

The NQT year can be difficult, suddenly you are responsible for a class or classes, teaching an almost full timetable, juggling getting to know your setting (if you're not lucky enough to secure a job in a placement school) and so on. All too often you might hear experienced teachers discussing how you just need to survive your NQT year. Forget that. Don't aspire to survive, aspire to thrive. I won't sugarcoat it: the first few years are hard. You're learning, developing and finding your feet. Just remember that teaching is a very personal affair so do it your way, teach proudly and love what you are doing, but don't be afraid to ask for help, guidance and support. Reach out when you need to.

Before I start writing a motivational speech, here are my top five tips for NQTs, which were originally shared on MrsHumanities.com.

1 Forget progress in the first half term

Honestly spend the first half term getting to know your students; how do they learn? What learning activities do they enjoy? What contributions do they make to school life? What hobbies do they have outside of school? Get to know the young people you are teaching. Build those all-important relationships and make it clear what your expectations are in the first term.

Personally, I wished I'd done exactly that during the first few weeks of my NQT year rather than worrying about whether students were making enough progress. I now like to spend the first half term finding out where my students are in regard to their subject knowledge, a bit about them and making my classroom expectations explicit. I make sure they are doing the little things that make the bigger things easier such as keeping their book tidy, meeting homework deadlines, bringing the correct equipment. If they are not doing those things I crack down on it immediately – detentions, phone calls home, no second chances. Sounds harsh, but it sets them up for the year.

2 Set up clear routines

My first school had a clear routine for students once they entered the classroom. Collect books, get out equipment, write the date, title and learning objective, underline them and then get on with the starter task until the register had been taken. This made it easy to set up initial routines. If your school doesn't have a specific start to lessons, create one. Students like consistency and knowing what to expect. Lay it out for them from day 1; you will have to repeat it a lot at first but eventually it sinks in.

However, it's not just the start of lessons you need to set up routines for. Consider routines for some of the following:

- End of lesson

- Peer/Self-assessment

- Class discussions

- Handing books out or collecting them in

- Borrowing equipment

- Toilet requests

The list could go on, but these will do for now.

3 Know your expectations

Ensure you know what you expect from your students before the first day of the job. It's important when setting the foundations with your classes that you are clear in relation to what you expect from them and what they can expect from you.

You will probably find yourself spending the first few weeks constantly repeating these rules and expectations but once your students are clear on them and are able to remember them (if you work in secondary, remember they will have numerous teachers with different expectations and routines so they won't instantly remember yours) you can then start to focus on the bigger picture – student progress.

Word of caution though: ensure your expectations are achievable – if students feel there is no way or chance of them meeting your expectations you'll likely be faced with some behavioural challenges.

4 Know the school rules

Consistency is important. Ensure you know and understand the school rules and behavioural routines before you start teaching. Firstly, it means students know what to expect if they consistently come up against the same routines. Also they can't argue back if you do what everyone else is (or should) be doing. Secondly it makes life in the classroom easier for you.

Ensure you give warnings clearly, set detentions and chase them up. Phone home if you must. Once students know they can't mess you around and that you are consistent, fair and follow through with sanctions then life in the classroom eventually becomes a little easier.

Overall be firm, be consistent and ensure that you and other NQTs know and follow the routines set out by the school.

5 Smile before Christmas

I'm sure you would have heard plenty of words of wisdom like the old "don't smile before Christmas". Ignore it. Greet your students on their way into your classroom and around the school. Talk to them off topic now and then. Tell them little snippets about yourself. Be human.

Personally, I tried too hard to be a 'teacher' in my first few years and not a human teaching other humans. I felt I had to be 100% the professional and didn't feel it was acceptable to share anything about myself with my students. I later realised this doesn't work; It makes you unapproachable and unrelatable.

Once you've established routines and expectations you can begin to relax a little with your students and let them see a bit of you – you're favourite colour (often related to the colour pen a student is using for their notes), your favourite parts of the topic (*insert excited face here* don't get me started on *insert topic*, I could talk about it for hours), your favourite books (oh, I see your reading . . . I love it, have you got to the part where. . . . Whoops, was that a spoiler?). I'm sure you get the picture. Have those conversations with your students; let them see you are human too.

If you're interested in further reading on the Teaching Standards and how to use them I highly recommend Geoff Barton's book 'Teach Now! The Essentials of Teaching'.

Takeaways

Demonstrating the teaching standards shouldn't have to feel like a chore during your training and NQT years. Develop strategies that allow you to show off what you do without it consuming large amounts of your time. Remember less is more.

Always reflect on the impact of your actions. Being a reflective practitioner is essential to developing your classroom practice and effectiveness.

Put your students at the forefront of everything you do in the classroom; consider the impact of your actions on them. Be human and smile before Christmas.

3 The challenges of the career

In my first five years, I almost made it into the statistic "a third of new teachers leave within the first five years", and it hasn't been just the once that I've wanted to pack up and leave the profession.

A personal perspective

My journey into teaching was somewhat bumpy. In fact, I'm surprised I made it past the first hurdle; the PGCE interview. During the interview I was asked the question "What is your biggest weakness?". Without really thinking about it I rather quickly gave my answer: "communication". Yes, communication! Probably not the best weakness to mention in an interview for a profession that relies on communication; but I was shy and introverted, so it was an honest answer. Instantly I regretted my answer though and I worried about it until I'd received my acceptance.

My next bump in the journey came from the fact that I undertook my PGCE at Aberystwyth University and had two placements some 30 miles from where I lived. Add to that the fact that I didn't drive at this point and relied on lifts and buses to get to and from my placement schools. Lugging folders and books home every day meant I built up some strong muscles though. This on top of the course took its toll; I was often exhausted, fed up and grumpy. I was not a good person to be around after the long bus journey home after the school day. Eventually, I attempted to leave the course in the Spring term, but my university mentor would not allow it; she believed in me too much.

To be blunt, the teacher training year is tough. You experience emotions you never felt possible, both highs and lows. You learn things about yourself that you never realised before. You become a different person, a teacher. By the time you reach the end of the school year, the holiday is needed. A break from all things school and education is required. Whether you have a job for September or not, you will probably find yourself longing to be back in the classroom. I know I did, even after wanting to leave the course.

The next way out of this adventure came towards the end of my PGCE year. I still hadn't secured a teaching job. I'd been very picky as I had been looking for jobs in South

East England, and travelling by train meant a journey of up to nine hours at times in one direction. In addition, I'd lost a lot of confidence during my second placement and felt I had to find the right school for me. When I moved down to the South East in the July, I took whatever job I could get and ended up working in a EYFS day nursery for nine months. It was big change from teaching secondary; however, I loved it.

I look back on the experience in the early year with fondness. It made me yearn for the classroom again. At first, I started to consider switching to primary as I found such pleasure in working with younger age groups; but really, I pined to teach my favourite subject, geography. I started to apply for teaching roles again and secured a job in a challenging secondary school. If you don't have a job for the next academic year, don't worry. Try supply or working in a different role for a period. The experience in EYFS rebooted my confidence and taught me a great deal about child development and how we learn to learn. Since then, I've implemented many strategies that I picked up from EYFS with Key Stage 3 and SEN students; some strategies have even gone beyond to Key Stage 4 and 5.

And that was all before even starting the main adventure, being a full-time teacher. The rest of the journey has had some monstrous challenges along with many sentimental moments of pride and success. It has been quite the rollercoaster. I've experienced stress, anxiety and depression as a direct result of the job. I've wanted to leave on many occasions. I've written numerous non-education job applications, formulated my resignation letter a few times and even printed it off once. That time I came extremely close to handing it in even though I didn't have another job lined up, reached the Headteacher's door but turned around.

Sadly, I'm not the only one. Government statistics from October 2016, showed that almost a third of new teachers that started teaching in England from 2010 left within five years. This equated to 13% of the 24,100 new teachers leaving by the end of the their NQT year, eventually making it to 30% by the end of five years. The pattern is similar for subsequent years.

If that isn't worrying enough, in the UK we also need *more* teachers. The numbers of teachers in secondary schools has fallen whilst the number of teachers leaving for reasons other than retirement has increased by 34,910 between 2011 and 2016. If we consider this alongside the shortfalls in ITT, the increase in uptake of EBacc subjects and rising pupil numbers, which are set to increase by 19.4% between 2017 and 2025 according to the Governments *Retaining and developing the teaching workforce report, January 2018*, then we have a crisis in the teaching profession.

But what makes teaching so challenging career that so many want to leave for reasons other than retirement?

Workload

Alongside increased accountability, performance management and scrutiny (to be discussed later in this chapter), more and more seems to be expected of teachers, both within the classroom and outside of it. The number of tasks we are expected to do in our working day aside from teaching individual lessons can become quite the size, so much of it burdensome and time consuming. As a result, in a UK classroom teachers work approximately 558 hours* outside of the annual 1265 hours of directed time. It is no surprise that so many have or are considering leaving the profession.

* calculations based on statistics from the Governments Teacher Workload Survey 2016 (Gibson et al., 2015)

At times I've felt like I'm supposed to be a miracle maker with the ability to create more time to fit work into. The most ironic request I've received that was outside of my day-to-day role was to create the schools' wellbeing policy, yet I was falling apart because I had none. Of course, being a pleaser and naive, I didn't say no at the time, but I did leave that school without ever having the time to work on it.

Now that I've made it through EYFS, my NQT year, two schools and being Head of Humanities I can confidently say that the thing I've found the hardest part of teaching is not the teaching itself. Too often, it's the workload: workload associated with covering our backs, to prove we are doing what we are doing and to demonstrate student progress to other people. And this is why we have a retention crisis in schools; the workload is excessive in comparison to our hours of directed time. We cannot effectively fulfil our job profiles within the working day. I'm not the only one to think this.

In 2014, the Department for Education conducted a review into teacher workload. The findings of the Workload Review (Gibson et al.,2015) confirmed that the two most burdensome of tasks were related to data and marking as stated by 56% and 53% of respondents. Other burdensome tasks included detailed planning, administration, meetings, reports, target setting and the implementation of change. All of this becomes unmanageable (Gibson et al., 2015).

In Dr Emma Kell's book, *How to Survive in Teaching*, in which she surveyed 3,864 teachers and education professionals, she states that when referring to the statement "my workload is manageable", 52% of respondents strongly disagreed, whilst another 28% disagreed. A total of 80% disagreed that their workload was manageable; this is unsustainable. Worse still is the stress, anxiety and in some cases depression that this is causing. Emma goes on to add that 82% of respondents that were practising teachers admit to experiencing anxiety directly related to the job, whilst 54% expressed that they experienced depression as a direct result.

This has been supported by the Education Support Partnerships Teacher Wellbeing Index 2018 report in which 67% of education professionals described themselves as stressed, 57% of which have considered leaving teaching over the past two years as a result of health pressures, followed by a further 72% citing that workload was their main reason for considering leaving. These figures are crazy, but not surprising.

Where does this workload come from?

In 2014, the NUT carried out a workload survey, they found that 80% of respondents said that school marking policies now cause excessive workload, 70% cited excessive data entry and analysis requirements as a cause of increased workload along with 62% point to Ofsted preparations and "Mocksteds". Other causes of workload were attributed to evidence for performance management purposes, unreasonable lesson planning requirements, observation and Department for Education initiatives.

Additionally, the Department for Education's research report 'Exploring teacher workload' published in March 2018, found the following to be causes of high levels of workload for both teachers and senior leaders

- Administration

- Behaviour monitoring and safeguarding

- Changing GCSE and A-Level specifications

- Data tracking

- Marking and assessment

- Planning and meetings

There are a few reoccurring themes on the cause of workload and burdensome tasks in schools: accountability, marking and assessment in addition to data analysis and reporting. The degree to which each theme influences workload varies between settings, but ultimately each has its influence and impact.

Accountability

Current accountability structures were introduced originally in 1988 as part of the Education Reform Act with the introduction of Ofsted and league tables, yet in my opinion Michael Gove's legacy had the most significant impact on teacher and school accountability. I was an NQT at the time so have little teaching experience prior to the Gove days, but I have seen the impact it has had on experienced professionals during this time.

Accountability is important to maintain virtuous standards of education for all. As teachers we have a responsibility and privilege to shape our student's futures, so of course there needs to be a level of scrutiny and accountability. But it's the way it has been implemented more recently and combined with performance-related pay that has impacted teachers and school leaders so negatively.

Ofsted and league tables have a widespread impact on teacher workload, wellbeing and stress. In my first two schools, I feel as though I heard the phrases 'for Ofsted' and 'Ofsted want' more than I heard the phrase "to benefit our students"; yet we are in our schools for our students. Everything we do should be for them, not for Ofsted, not for the LA, not for the Headteacher or the MAT boss, but for the students in our care.

There are many examples from schools across the country whereby strategies have been implemented not for the benefit of students, whether directly or indirectly, but instead to tick a box in preparation for Ofsted. These are strategies that have had little to no benefit for the students. So why were we doing them in the first place?

Despite Ofsted and league tables, for teachers it appears to be the introduction of performance-related pay and the associated accountability that has increased workload, stress and mental health concerns the most.

In 2013, the Department for Education released details on how schools will be able to link teachers' pay to performance, allowing them to pay good teachers more. By September 2013 schools had to revise their pay and appraisal policies to outline how pay progression would be linked to teacher's performance. The advice suggested schools assess teachers on their performance in some of the following ways:

- Their impact on pupil progress

- Their impact on wider outcomes for pupils

- Their contribution to improvements in other areas (e.g. pupils' behaviour or lesson planning)

- Their commitment to professional and career development

- Their wider contribution to the work of the school, for instance their involvement in school business outside the classroom

For many this has meant the creation of pupil progress targets, specific targets for performance in observations and the passing of inspections of different kinds across the year. It has also led to the lack of autonomy in the performance management process for many as well signification levels of micro-management for some.

Some of the most challenging targets I've been given have included the following:

- Minimum of 90% of students to achieve A-C grades

- All students in a class to achieve 2 or more levels of progress

- All pupils and groups are expected to make 4–6 points of progress during the academic year

■ To deliver a minimum of three good or outstanding lessons through formal observation where one observation has to be outstanding

■ To achieve a minimum of six good or outstanding work judgements in book scrutinizes, where one is to be outstanding across a range of books from the classes in which you are responsible.

■ To deliver one INSET and one twilight session per academic year

Of the targets above, those in which I had to demonstrate a value-added score, or specific levels of progress, were the hardest and most stressful to achieve. If I'm honest it made me more lenient in my marking. If a student were appearing as underperforming in our data programme with a bright red box, I'd up the sublevel of the levelled grade, from 4c to 4a, and there you have it, a nice green box. Did it impact student progress? Not at all. Did these targets impact my teaching? Most certainly.

The implementation of such specific targets, some of which are impossible to achieve due to external factors, has massively increased the stress experienced by teachers to perform. It has also led to a greater amount of micro-management to facilitate others to meet their personal targets.

At the same time, the level of scrutiny many teachers and leaders now experience has grown exponentially, diminishing trust and autonomy further.

But a lot of schools are changing the way in which they set performance management targets, making them personal and developmental rather than stringent and hard to achieve. However, we do need more schools making this change.

Ofsted

Ofsted can be seen as an entirely separate beast of accountability. The state school inspectorate creates a sense of fear and stress for teachers and school leaders alike. Before its removal, it judged teachers on their performance during a snapshot observation. On occasions hardworking, dedicated teachers were deemed 'inadequate' simply because they didn't 'perform' on the day. The stress and impact of such judgements can ruin careers. Fortunately, I've not been on the receiving end of that experience. But I know of others that have, many of which weren't given support from their schools and ultimately made the decision to leave teaching for good.

My first school received a visit from Ofsted in the first term, not long before the October break. I was a bag of nerves throughout the visit. I was observed, not necessarily with a class I would have chosen, but it went well, and I received a 'good with outstanding features' judgement. Not bad for just seven weeks of teaching. Yet, by the end of it I was beyond exhausted. I'd worked until late at night meticulously planning each lesson over the two-day period, documenting student progress, worrying about behaviour of some of the classes that I could be observed with. Everyone worked so hard for the outstanding judgement the school received overall; yet we all worked incredibly hard every day in the lead-up and every day afterwards in preparation for the next scrutiny or Ofsted visit. My second school was very similar. We were constantly in anticipation for Ofsted. Constantly preparing, waiting and stressing. Nobody wants to deliberately let the team down.

It's refreshing working in a school that doesn't fear Ofsted, that doesn't keep referring to what Ofsted wants to see in every staff meeting. That wants to explore and embed evidence-based practice – strategies that have research and evidence behind them. This may just be a sign of the times and reflective of societal changes in education, or it could just be the leadership in which I now work under. Either way it's refreshing not to keep hearing the phrase "Ofsted". I hope more schools are moving away from second guessing what the inspectorate wants to see, particularly with the publication of the 'Ofsted inspections: myths' document which outlines what the inspectorate does not expect to see, check or require with the occasional clarification on what they will do or discuss.

With the clarification and change coming from Ofsted, it is now time for schools to move away from striving to please the inspectorate. Although admittedly, it's harder said than done for schools to be judged less than 'good', and instead to focus on the development and implementation of good practice that works for them, their staff and students.

Marking and assessment

Marking and feedback has become a monstrous task for many with strategies such as triple marking, recording of verbal feedback and the expectation of extensive written comments and dialogue between students and the teacher. For many marking has become a chore they'd rather not face.

However, providing high-quality feedback is integral to effective teaching and learning. Marking and checking books allows us as teachers to assess how well pupils have learnt the topic, skill or content covered. The assessment of students should then feed into planning to address misconceptions and ensure the level of challenge is reflective of student capabilities. The Sutton Trust-EEF Teaching and Learning Toolkit "suggests that the provision of high-quality feedback can lead to an average of eight additional months' progress over the course of a year" (Higgins et al., 2014), demonstrating its importance. Yet so many schools are doing it wrong. Instead of supporting progress and effective planning, it's become a time consuming all-encompassing task that many teachers would rather not do.

Developing a marking and feedback toolkit is essential to assessment and planning. Building up a range of go-to strategies that you implement regularly and form the basis of your lessons and feedback is key to maximising the time you have available.

Over the last few years, marking and feedback has been high on my agenda. I've researched, trialled and implemented a variety of feedback strategies with the sole aim of ensuring high-quality feedback for my students and a reduced workload for me. I feel I can safely say I've been successful at finding what works for me, my students and my setting and have set about implementing some of the successful routines and strategies into my department's feedback approach to reduce our marking workload.

In addition to the workload from marking, the frequency of assessment and data points throughout the year has a damning impact on workload. Sometimes I think senior leaders forget the impact both on students and staff of frequent testing and assessment. In my last school, a data drop occurred the week before every half term. This meant an assessment of achievement and progress for every student I taught that amounted to more than ten classes, across 5-year groups. The workload from assessment was too much. Schools that have reduced the regularity of assessment and data points in the school year have helped to reduce the associated workload. It also supports effective planning and distribution of feedback and assessment to reduce the number of crunch points that teachers experience.

Data analysis and reporting

At first it can be challenging to understand the data we create and hold on our students; yet we are told to create and use it, and that data is required to understand a student's starting point and progress.

Yet with changes to examinations and the removal of national curriculum levels at primary and Key Stage 3 as part of the Government's assessment reforms combined with the variety of approaches now being used by schools, preparing new teachers to understand and effectively use data is even harder.

Since my first teaching post in 2012, I've used the following data on pupils to understand their starting points and to assess their progress

- Cognitive Abilities Test scores

- GCSE grades A*-F

- GCSE grades 1–9 for KS4

- GCSE grades 1–9 dropped down to KS3

- IBDP grades and essay mark bands

- Internal baseline test scores

- Internally created mastery levels

- Levels from Standard Assessment Tests

- MYP levels

- National Curriculum Levels

- Point scores

- Predicted grades

- Prior attainment banding

- Target grades

- Value-added scores

The only training I've received on understanding any of this data was during my PGCE, and we looked at using the National Curriculum levels. Even then we only learned how to interpret and make use of the level descriptors to assess student attainment. Understanding this data has to be self-taught, and I only do as much with it as is requested of me. I'd rather spend the time putting learning first.

To put learning first I make time to assess, interpret and understand my students' knowledge of the subject, their ability to apply that knowledge and to teach them in a way that ensures they make good progress. I identify their starting points within the subject and stretch and challenge them to succeed. I can assess them if they are making sufficient progress, otherwise I need to intervene to support them further. I put learning first because my problem with data stems from the fact that I believe students are not test scores or pieces of data. Data doesn't give you the full picture of a student's past, present and future attainment. It doesn't consider external influences, and too often its used to hold teachers accountable. I'd rather identify if a student is making good progress or not and what is being done to ensure they do.

Yet understanding and using data isn't the only challenge. Often teachers are asked to complete data and reporting tasks that do not necessarily directly inform or improve teaching or student outcomes. These tasks sometimes involve the use of complex software that increases the time spent inputting or analysing data. For instance, my second school used 4Matrix for data analysis. As a subject leader it was my responsibility to make use of the software to analyse student progress. It'd take me longer to find the appropriate information than it would to analyse it because it wasn't used frequently enough to embed the process. Even though I understood the value of the software to track student progress, its complexity and infrequent use meant it added to my already heavy workload.

Then there is also the frequency of data reporting. For instance, half termly or termly assessments for individual pupils might not just be a grade, level or score but might entail more specific learning objectives within subjects. These are then analysed by teachers, subject leaders, heads of year or other school leaders and may feed into regular reporting to parents, individual written reports and parent consultation evenings. This often leads to duplicative systems that increase workload, stress and discontent.

The schools that have reduced reporting to parents are changing how data is used. Data drops and reduced assessment of students are leading the way in workload reduction. It is possible to deliver high-quality education without a burdensome workload for staff.

Other challenges

Unfortunately, though, workload is not the only factor that is driving teachers to leave. Other challenges include behaviour, poor work-life balance and the public perception of teachers and schools. Let's take a little look at each.

Behaviour

In 2014, Education Support Partnership carried out research into behaviour. From the survey they found that "almost one in four teachers complained that behaviour was preventing them from teaching effectively". Whilst from a primary teacher perspective, 62% of teachers said that poor behaviour had resulted in stress, anxiety or depression with 37% considering leaving as a result of behaviour problems.

Dealing with negative behaviour in the classroom can be exhausting on its own. To then have to carry out sanctions such as teacher-led detentions is onerous and burdensome. The number of break and lunch times I've given over to detentions in the past is uncountable; worst still is the number of one-hour after school detentions I've had to supervise after school in non-directed time. I wasn't even a member of school leadership.

Non-centralised detentions increase the burden on teachers to give up their time when they should be taking a break from the school day. They also encourage teachers to not enforce such sanctions, which means that disciplinary issues are not always addressed.

In addition to setting and supervising sanctions comes the record-keeping of misdemeanours and sanctions. The paper trail, the phone calls to home and the follow ups. And if you haven't the support of the school leadership team or consistency in application across the school, it can leave classroom teachers with a time bill they didn't ask for.

The work-life juggle

There are multiple examples of ways teachers are trying to balance their work-life and home-life from family commitments like children or sick relatives to social engagements like weddings, family gatherings and other events. Juggling work and life in a profession that spills out into potentially every hour of your waking day is difficult.

Mrs Humanities
@MrsHumanities

If there's one thing I've learnt from burnout and breakdown it's don't let teaching consume you. You have to step back, relax and let the teacher guilt passover you. Don't open the door and let it in, otherwise it gets comfortable and pushes your wellbeing out. #love2teach

1:19 AM - 17 Aug 2018

50 Retweets **302** Likes

💬 13   🔁 50   ♡ 302   ılı

Figure 3.1 Twitter quote

In my initial years of teaching, the thought of organising a wedding or having children terrified me. Some weeks I wouldn't find the time to wash my hair (thank goodness for dry shampoo) let alone get someone else dressed, fed and off to nursery or school. Now that I've managed to balance work and life better, the prospect of having both a career and life is far more plausible. Unfortunately for many, this has not been the case, and leaving the profession has been the only option for them.

The worst and most challenging part of the work-life juggle though in my opinion is the 'teacher guilt' when you do spend time on yourself, whether it be during the school week, weekend or even during holidays. It's a pang of regret that we should be doing something school related: marking those books, planning that lesson, sending that email or contacting that parent. If you open the door for guilt, it can get into every corner of the mental abyss of our minds. It can be a contributing factor to burnout and breakdown as we allow it to take away our sense of self, and as we put the needs and demands of our work before our own. It encourages us to live as a teacher rather than work as a teacher.

We must make time for our hobbies, our interests and our families. We cannot be martyrs; we must not compete for the most hours worked. We must fight for a reasonable balance.

Problematic parents

I experienced a number of problematic parents during my first five years of teaching.

One particular example I experienced was as an NQT. I was being bullied by one parent of a particularly troublesome student. Every time I had to call home regarding the negative behavioural choices of their child, I'd spend a good half an hour or sometimes longer psyching myself up for the call. I would write down exactly what I would say and rehearse it, and then finally would gather up the confidence to make that call. After a particularly explosive incident from the parent, I was no longer allowed to contact home for that student and instead had to pass the issue onto my subject leader or SLT. The stress and anxiety associated with not only teaching that student but having to deal with the consequences of their choices, I imagine, was beyond their parent's imagination. Yet all I wanted was for their child and for those in their class to succeed.

Parents want the best for their children as do we, but that doesn't always mean they understand our perspective. Sometimes, parents can be a great cause of stress, anxiety and workload for teachers and school leaders. Getting parents to support teachers is vital for any school but it isn't always easy.

Challenging colleagues

On the odd occasion, there can be the challenging colleague. Fortunately, I've not experienced this to the extreme that I know others have. There are many stories of bullying, incompetence and critical colleagues that simply add to the day-to-day stresses of the job.

If you ever find yourself on the receiving end of such a colleague, ensure you talk to someone about it whether it be your line manager, SLT or a union representative. It's vital that you raise the issue, keep note of events and pass on concerns.

Reputation & responsibility

And after all of that, there's the public image that teachers and schools have. If you speak to the public, teachers and schools generally fall into one of three narratives

1   Teachers have thirteen weeks paid holiday. Our working hours are between 9 am to 3 pm. Essentially, schools are a rather cheap babysitting service that just cause a huge amount of grief for parents.

2   Teaches need to make students succeed, and schools need to ail all of society's ills. Schools should be keeping students in school, so parents can work longer. Teachers need to be teaching students not just subjects but preparing them for adulthood. Teachers and schools should be counsellors, mental health advisors, sexual health clinics, food banks etc.

3   Teachers work hard for their students; the hours are long, and we are committed to doing what we can to support our students to thrive in their educational escapades.

I like to imagine everyone feels teachers fall into the latter, but unfortunately, I know that is wishful thinking. There are ever increasing demands being placed on schools, leaders and teachers from parents, businesses, universities and the government, and whilst we are expected to do more than just educate our students in academic content, we are expected to do it with tighter budgets, fewer staff and greater accountability.

> ### Opportunity to think
>
> What do find most challenging about teaching?
> What would help to improve the situation?
> What elements do you have control of that you can change?

But hope is on the horizon

Already since my breakdown in 2016, I've seen positive action being taken to support new and experienced teachers nationally and within schools, including my current workplace.

Organisations such as the Education Support Partnership, the Anna Freud National Centre for Children and Families and the Teach Well Alliance, along with the teaching unions, are working to raise awareness of the implications stress, high workload and accountability is having on teachers, support staff and school leaders across the UK. In doing so, the Department for Education, Ofsted and school leaders are listening to what classroom teachers have to say.

For instance, following the launch of the Workload Challenge in October 2014, the DfE established the Independent Teacher Workload Review Groups which have reported on and suggested solutions to the unnecessary burdens associated with marking, planning and data management. As a result, in July 2018, the DfE released the *Workload Reduction Toolkit*, which are a set of resources providing practical advice and tools to enable school leaders and teachers to review and reduce workload. Now we need school leaders to take the positive steps to reduce unnecessary workload within their schools, without the fear of Ofsted inspections and associated judgements that may deter from such changes.

Saying that though, it's not just down to those in charge of our schools. We as individuals and teams are gaining confidence in our ability to mobilise and act to create change in our own schools, and are working together to create a better environment for staff and students. We can take our own action to manage our workload and wellbeing, which will be discussed in more detail in later chapters.

Additionally, as a result of recognising the challenges associated with teaching, many ITT providers are now providing increased support and guidance for those now entering the profession to enable new teachers to survive and thrive during training, induction and onwards as advised by the DfE in the *Addressing teacher workload in Initial Teacher Education (ITE)* report published in November 2018.

Burnouts and breakdowns are not a rite of passage in becoming a great teacher. Long hours, burnout, stress, anxiety, discontent . . . the story doesn't have to be that way. Find a school that values teacher wellbeing, that works to provide staff with a work-life balance and that actively engages with staff to create that balance. There are many schools out there that are already embedding this and many more that are taking the plunge to make it that way. Find them or help create them.

Takeaways

Teaching is a challenging career, yet as cliché as it is, it really is extremely rewarding. And the best part is I can see a wave of change on the horizon as teachers, school leaders and other organisations raise awareness of the impacts of the profession on teachers' health and wellbeing. As more of us raise the issue and its subsequent impact on recruitment and retention, people are listening: the Government and Ofsted, ITT programme leaders and parents, and at times even the media. This is leading to positive change for our profession. The emphasis towards less is more is arising, and the profession's work-life balance is starting to recuperate. Now all we need are brave and determined school leaders, middle leaders and even individual teachers to continue to insist on and incorporate workload-reducing changes in their schools.

If you're reading this as a trainee, NQT or early-career teacher, you've got a lot to look forward to. Stick with it when times are hard, reach out for support and guidance when you need to and enjoy the moments of bliss when they occur. Top tip, when students are working independently, step back and take it in; remember those moments when you need to.

References

Department for Education (2016) *School workforce in England: November 2015* [pdf] Department for Education. Available at https://assets.publishing.service.gov.uk/government/uploads/system/uploads/attachment_data/file/533618/SFR21_2016_MainText.pdf [Accessed 4th April 2018]

Department for Education (2018) *Exploring teacher workload: Qualitative research: Research report March 2018* [pdf] Department for Education. Available at https://assets.publishing.service.gov.uk/government/uploads/system/uploads/attachment_data/file/686734/Exploring_teacher_workload.pdf [Accessed 12th May 2018]

Education Support Partnership (2014) *Behaviour survey* [Online] Available at www.educationsupportpartnership.org.uk/resources/research-reports/behaviour-survey

Education Support Partnership (2018) *Education support partnerships teacher wellbeing index 2018* [pdf] Available at www.educationsupportpartnership.org.uk/sites/default/files/teacher_wellbeing_index_2018.pdf [Accessed 23rd October 2018]

Gibson, S. et al. (2015) Workload challenge: Analysis of teacher consultation responses: Research report: February 2015 [pdf] Available at https://assets.publishing.service.gov.uk/government/uploads/system/uploads/attachment_data/file/401406/RR445_-_Workload_Challenge_-_Analysis_of_teacher_consultation_responses_FINAL.pdf [Accessed 12th May 2018]

Higgins, S., Katsipataki, M., Kokotsaki, D., Coleman, R., Major, L. E., & Coe, R. (2014) *The Sutton Trust-Education Endowment Foundation Teaching and Learning Toolkit*. London: Education Endowment Foundation.

House of Commons (2018) Retaining and developing the teaching workforce: Seventeenth report of session 2017–2019 [pdf] Available at https://publications.parliament.uk/pa/cm201719/cmselect/cmpubacc/460/460.pdf [Accessed 21st July 2018]

Kell, E. (2018) *How to Survive in Teaching Without Imploding, Exploding or Walking Away.* Bloomsbury Education, London, UK.

NUT (2014) *Teachers and workload* [pdf] National Union of Teachers. Available at www.teachers.org.uk/files/teachers-and-workload-survey-report-september-2014.pdf [Accessed 12th May 2018]

4 Staying in the profession

Despite the workload and stresses, there are many reasons to love and remain in the profession. Sometimes we need to take a moment to remember why we love teaching and what attracted us to it in the first place.

Opportunity to think

What do you love most about teaching?
How does standing in front of an engaged class of students make you feel?
What has learning to teach taught you?
Do you enjoy the variety of each day?
Do you find teaching fulfilling?
What would you be doing if you weren't teaching?

Whenever anyone asks me about why I stay in teaching, I'm reminded of those moments in the classroom when everything just clicks, my students are thinking and working hard, and I can step back and take it all in. In those moments I feel a sense of serenity before a rush of excitement. It's those moments that made me love the classroom and change my career aspirations.

Other reasons I love teaching

- Every student is different, each with their own personality, strengths and weaknesses.

- Every student you teach makes each day different; it's never the same. Even when I teach the same content to classes in the same year group the class dynamics vary the experience.

- The lightbulb moments: when a student finally gets it, their eyes light up and a smile creeps across their face. I love seeing that moment.

- Ingenuity of students: whether it's the creative homework project, the excuses for not doing their homework or their approach towards a difficult task, students always surprise me with their creativity, their inventive approaches and their resourcefulness.

- We get to influence the futures of so many young people; we can inspire, change, and influence. That's an important role and responsibility; we are creating the global citizens of the future. I want my students to be the best person they can possibly be.

Yet, I often forget this when I've had a difficult day or a challenging series of days, weeks or months. But even then, something keeps me here. A sense of commitment that in the past has led to a downfall in my health and wellbeing because all too often, we feel tied to a school even when we are struggling. We form relationships with colleagues and students, and we want the best for them.

However, if our wellbeing and mental health is suffering we have to make a change. Whether it be creating change in your current setting by offering alternatives to the way things are being done or whether it means changing your setting entirely by moving schools. You can't just keep doing what you are doing and hope for a different outcome. It's important to look after yourself evident by my cautionary experience.

Staying in the profession: my experience

For two years I'd worked tirelessly and reached a point when I was on the verge of walking from teaching. I'd reached rock bottom and struggled to remember what I loved about the job.

I took time off in April 2016 and I thought that was going to be the end of my time in the classroom. After a few days off, I eventually rang the Education Support Partnership who gave me the confidence to ask for professional help. I started on anti-depressants, opened up to my family and finally acknowledged my position and my choices; I could either stay or leave.

I decided that I'd give one more school a try. This would be my third. I was encouraged to write an application for a position at a top school in the area. I was invited for interview whilst I was still signed off sick which worried me. Despite still struggling on the day of interview I went and did what I loved; I taught geography.

I really liked the school. I asked about how the school supported staff wellbeing in the interview and was happy with the response. But I still worried. I worried my time off would look bad. I worried that this school would be the same; it would have high expectations of staff with limited time to meet those expectations, regular inspections, Mocksteds, frequent observations and so on. But I really wanted to stay in teaching. I loved it.

I was offered the job almost immediately, but I needed time to think. They were happy to give it to me. I'd be leaving behind a department I'd built up from nothing (literally), single-handed. My physical and mental health had gone into that department and the school, every resource and every lesson. I'd be leaving behind a major part of me. But when I spoke to the current Headteacher to explain my predicament, I knew then I was replaceable, barely valued. My decision was made for me. I accepted the job offer, and it's been the best decision.

I still take anti-depressants. I tried coming off of them, and even though I'm so much happier, manage my time effectively and absolutely love teaching again I can't cope with the general anxiety of the role. I went back on them after just a few weeks. Whilst I may still experience high levels of stress and anxiety at times, the experience has enabled me to better manage it. It has made me more aware and supportive of the mental health of others and better at managing and dealing with the challenges of the career.

If my experience sounds anything like yours, at any point in your teaching career, know you are not alone and never will be. There's more information on the help and support available as well as on what to look out for in Chapter 11.

Are you putting your wellbeing at risk?

If you're not sleeping well, working many hours beyond directed time, rarely finding the time to see family and friends, you might be putting your wellbeing at risk. Perhaps you're regularly feeling stressed and anxious about work too.

Take a step back and evaluate your position. Consider is it teaching, your job or the school?

For me, moving schools was my solution, but it's just one of many. Personally, I would say don't settle until you find the school for you. Yes, you build relationships with students and staff, but in the end, it is just a job and if the job is making you unhappy, change the situation. The following provides suggestions to help you change your situation without having to leave teaching.

Staying in teaching: the importance of the right school

It can be daunting leaving a school you have come to know, a school where you feel comfortable, a school where you feel a commitment to the students and staff. Too often, the choice becomes stay there or leave altogether. This truly saddens me.

If you are unhappy at the school where you are employed, do not let yourself be convinced that all schools are the same. They aren't. The leadership and community of a school can make a big difference to your wellbeing and workload. If you love teaching, try other schools before deciding to step away.

My first two schools were challenging in so many ways; the high expectations of staff, the behaviour, the workload etc., and before applying for the job at my current school I was terrified it would be more of the same. For me it was a period of do I stay, or do I go.

I decided to give one more school a go, and it worked out. I feel appreciated, supported and valued by both staff and students, and that makes an enormous difference.

If you decide to apply for positions at other schools, consider asking about workload, the average hours worked and more importantly how they support staff wellbeing. Don't just ask this to the interview panel, ask the teachers you meet. Doing so will give you a feel for the school and the value placed on staff wellbeing and their work-life balance.

Staying in teaching: the options

1 Supply teaching

Although you are not necessarily guaranteed hours, supply teaching can open you up to a variety of schools you may not have considered in the past. Supply teaching can give you the opportunity to experience other schools, to find out what ticks your boxes and pushes your buttons. Time to discover what other schools are doing well and where you wouldn't want to return. In addition, through supply you also avoid some of the additional stresses of a permanent position such as marking, assessment and reporting, which may lead you to teach without the added pressures and responsibilities.

> Laura Braun was an acting deputy headteacher at the time of her illuminating realisation; she was persistently working, spending just half a day on weekends with family. Additionally, the stress had built up and she started experiencing panic attacks until eventually she left her position and school.
>
> Laura didn't want to leave teaching but wanted more time with her family. She did a year of PPA cover and supply teaching whilst she considered her options. During her time as a supply teacher she found the 'perfect' school and was offered a position. At first, she politely declined as she didn't feel she was mentally in the right place. However, after some time and some kind persistence from the school, she accepted the offer so long as she only worked four days a week; Laura has now been at this school since September 2017 and is much happier with her work-life balance.

2 Primary to secondary

Moving from primary to secondary can be a challenge unto itself. Very few teachers make the move up. An applicant's ability to demonstrate sufficient subject knowledge to teach across a minimum of Key Stage 3 and 4 is essential.

However, with the range of shortage subjects and/or recruitment difficulties in some areas of the country, if you are willing to adapt and possibly move this will enhance your chances.

Coming from primary may put applicants in good stead for being able to offer additional subjects dependent on qualifications and experience, as well as to teach in Key Stage 3 and year 6 to year 7 transition.

In making this move, you may wish to consider undertaking subject knowledge enhancement courses such as those offered online by the TES (www.tes.com/institute/subject-knowledge-enhancement-teachers).

3 Secondary to primary

Moving from secondary to primary is far more prevalent. In making this move, teachers convert from being a specialist to a generalist, teaching one class most of the time. This must be carefully considered.

The competition can be fierce when you are competing against primary qualified applicants, so it is vital to demonstrate your commitment to primary education. Therefore, if considering this route, you may wish to undertake some formal training in primary education such as a SKE course in primary maths or

Before applying for primary vacancies is there the possibility of undertaking a few days in a primary setting? Read up on the primary curriculum and explore ways of teaching reading, phonics and basic numeracy across the ability spectrum.

Consider what your experience in secondary can bring to a primary setting, perhaps you've worked with transition to year 7 or Key Stage 5. Have you done any specific work in additional educational needs? Perhaps you could enter into primary as a subject specialist.

If a full move to primary isn't possible or seems daunting, consider middle schools or independent prep-schools that teach children aged 8 to 13.

Holly Dyson was a teacher of English and History that transitioned from secondary to primary. After a horrific experience which led to a decline in her mental health and resignation Holly took up a role as a supply teacher with a local agency. This meant she could look for jobs outside of teaching but still have some income in the meantime. She intended to return to library work which she had done before teacher training. However with the support from her doctor, family and the Education Support team she was helped to find her love for education again.

During supply work, she found that every single school had a unique situation each with its different pressures and seemingly, expectations. She worked on a long-term supply position and it helped her to get back to the basics of teaching. She was given the opportunity to work with primary age children and soon found her feet again. Quickly she was told that she was a great teacher and hearing those words allowed her to open up and trust again. Trust teaching, education and above all, herself.

4 Independent schools

This may not be for everyone; there are still many stresses involved with teaching in Independent schools, but they are different to what you mind find in the state sector. Things such as Saturday schools, longer weekdays and additional duties may put people offer, but since they are independent and free from government intervention, independent schools are free to decide what and how they teach, meaning there is greater curriculum freedom and non-compulsory testing.

Find out more about independent schools at www.isc.co.uk/

Tracey Wilson is now a Headteacher, after having experienced the pressure and work-load associated with an ambitious Head striving for an Outstanding Ofsted she felt like leaving in just her second year of teaching at primary level.

Instead Tracy made the jump from the state sector to Independent. Upon leaving the state school, she was told she "wasn't up to the job" yet within four years had made it to Headship. She loves the renewed freedom she experienced in the Independent sector and highly recommends it as a possibility for others.

5 Prep and middle schools

Not as widely found in the UK as others school types, but if you're in the right area or willing to move, a prep or middle school maybe an option. In addition to the freedoms for independent schools, class sizes tend to smaller and curriculum taught by subject rather than key-stage specialists.

You can find out more on prep and middle schools at http://iaps.uk/

6 Further education

If you decide FE is an option, as a qualified school teacher there is nothing to stop you from applying for FE roles since ITT qualifications are fully recognised in this sector.

There are a variety of options at FE, you may wish to continue to teach your specialist subject or there is the opportunity to move to this sector and focus on skills such literacy and numeracy, ESOL or SEN. With the latter areas of study, you may be required to undertake further qualification in preparation or as part of the role. The Education and Training Foundation website (www.feadvice.org.uk) has plenty of information to support the move to FE.

There are few jobs that are quite as scrutinised as teaching, but it doesn't need to be a point of stress and fear. In her second year as an English teacher, Gemma Jones struggled with what she felt was constant scrutiny. It dented her confidence and made me feel powerless. However rather than let it consume her until she left, she took some of the power back by seeking out a mentor.

She sought an inspirational teacher and humbled herself enough to ask them to mentor her. As a result, she reflected upon her practice, acknowledged her strengths and weaknesses and challenged herself to develop.

Having a mentor allowed her to reaffirm that she was a hardworking teacher, consistently striving for her best and what scrutiny process could argue with that? She felt in control again.

Gemma recognised that developing an interest in teaching and learning pedagogy gave her confidence and a lifeline. She later moved to FE and has found that scrutiny and pressure is well managed, less frequent and more useful.

7 SEN

Since there is currently no postgraduate teacher training route in to SEN teaching, many of those teaching in SEN schools make the move from mainstream primary or secondary settings. To improve your chances, you may wish to undertake a course or two in specialist education. The SEN Magazine advertises a wide range of up-to-date listing of CPD opportunities in SEN (https://senmagazine.co.uk/cpd/cpd/cpd-listings)

Vicky Frohnsdorff-Harris is now an SEN teacher, after having been Head of Music at a secondary school. Vicky burnt out after leading a one-person department in a large school where she had to rely on untrained staff to fulfil the remaining timetabled lessons. She eventually left and joined an Independent Prep school however her experience wasn't exactly a positive one there either. Eventually Vicky decided to take a different route and took up a temporary post in a SEN school teaching Key Stage 1. Despite taking a large pay cut, she now feels like she's making a real difference which has been recognised by SLT.

Vicky's experience taught her that if you're not enjoying your job, then your pupils suffer. She is now much stricter about how much time she spends working outside of directed time to ensure she doesn't miss out on family time and is the most effective teacher she can be.

8 Change subject

I envisage an issue for retaining staff in foundation subjects arising as a result of the English Baccalaureate. With the focus on core subjects building and the diminishing value of the foundation subjects that do not comprise the EBacc, more and more of these teachers will feel underappreciated or will no longer be required. If you teach such subjects or your falling out of love with your specialist subject you may want to consider enhancing the subjects you can teach or change your subject entirely. The subject knowledge enhancement course previously mentioned will be helpful in developing your understanding of subjects outside of your professionalism.

9 Reduce your hours

In 2014, the flexible working regulations were amended in the UK. This means that all employees have the right to request flexible working after twenty-six weeks of employment with their employer.

In teaching this may involve requesting a reduction of your hours from full-time to part-time, flexitime around core hours, a degree of homeworking during PPA and frees or a job share.

If you can afford to, you may wish to consider reducing your hours to provide yourself with more time for the work-life juggle.

If reducing your hours is a possibility, there is a legal procedure that must be followed as detailed below.

1   Put your request into writing, including the specified changes that you applied for and the proposed date to which changes will come into effect. Try to include how this might impact the school and how it might be dealt with.

2   The employer must respond with the decision within three months of the application.

3   Employees have fourteen days to appeal against any refusal to the request.

If you'd like to find out more on flexible working, the teaching unions and department for education have plenty of information available to support your application.

Here are some links to get you started

ATL www.atl.org.uk/advice-and-resources/publications/flexible-working
NASUWT www.nasuwt.org.uk/advice/conditions-of-service/flexible-working.html
NUT www.teachers.org.uk/help-and-advice/self-help/f/flexible-working
Department for Education www.gov.uk/government/publications/flexible-working-
  in-schools

Sarah Larsen was Head of Geography when she decided she wanted to be able to spend sufficient quality time with her family and first born. Sarah didn't want to leave the profession but knew she could no longer work full-time. She emailed her Headteacher to ask to step down from her position and reduce her hours to three days a week. This request was accepted, allowing her to spend time with her daughter whilst staying in the classroom.

When she then had her second daughter, Sarah chose to leave teaching for a while. When both children were in full-time education, she began to think about returning to the classroom in some capacity. Originally, she looked for teaching assistant positions, but was convinced to contact her old school. Sarah found herself in the fortunate position that they needed someone to fill some gaps in the geography timetable, but only for one academic year. That was six years ago.

Even though the first couple of years were tough, having to start again as a new teacher in a familiar school, and was a steep learning curve, Sarah believes it's one of the best decisions she's ever made! Returning part-time has allowed her to gain her independence again after starting a family, to continue with the job she loves and still be there for her own children.

10 Reducing responsibility

If you're struggling with the workload or feeling stressed by responsibility associated with a TLR, it might be necessary to step down from the position to classroom teacher. Although it can be a process that brings a sense of failure, making the decision requires strength. It takes further strength to inform your line manager or employer of your decision. Do not feel like you have failed if you decide to step down from a position of responsibility and instead use it as an opportunity to develop and refine your classroom practice to enhance your work-life balance.

Katie Hilton, a geography teacher felt that in her second year the workload, marking expectations, lack of support from SLT was too much. As a result, she resigned and temporarily stepped down as a teacher, taking on the role of an HLTA at a SEN school.

Working as a HLTA meant that Katie had the opportunity to continue teaching a variety of subjects, allowing her to develop her pedagogical practice without the stress of being the main teacher. She was later offered a part-time role, four days a week and in a much smaller school.

After one year of being back in the classroom Katie believes she found a school that fit her. For her that meant she found an SLT that was incredibly supportive of their staff and students.

11 International teaching

This can be a trickier move to make, particularly if you have dependents, but it is possible. A teaching qualification from the UK is often transferable to other countries, and there are many possible routes you can take to teach abroad.

If you wish to continue teaching in a style that you are used to, international schools are a possible alternative. As a qualified teacher from the UK, it is unlikely international schools will demand any extra qualifications. Additionally, British international schools usually use English as their main language and often make use of the British curriculum, qualifications and exam boards meaning a sense of familiarity abroad.

In addition, there can be other benefits to teaching abroad including smaller class sizes, allowances such as housing and travel allowance, time and money for professional development and in some cases tax-free salaries.

Tom Rogers had been a teacher for eight years and Head of History at a UK school before he lost faith in the British education system in its current form. In the UK, he'd found that teaching was a lifestyle rather than a job, resulting in him becoming a ghost of his former self. He took the difficult decision to leave the profession in December 2015, but before he knew it, he was yearning to be back in the classroom.

In September 2016, Tom took up the post of Head of History at a British International School in Spain. Tom found an amazing school, with great facilities, a friendly and welcoming staff and a commitment to a holistic education without the pressure of Ofsted, leagues tables and workload. The climate also helped him to settle in.

He now lives and teaches in Slovenia, having started a job as assistant headteacher at the British International School of Ljublyana in January 2019. Alongside his day job, he coordinates TMHistoryIcons and writes for the TES.

Alternatively, become a rebel teacher

I only really started to make a change to my workload when I started to rebel a bit against the systems and policies in place. I wanted to keep my employer happy and I wanted to be the best that I could be, yet I was unhappy and needed to see change. If no one was going to change things in the school, I'd make the change happen myself.

At first it was only mild rebellion; marking took up most of my free time and I only wanted to reduce it to give me more time to do other tasks that needed to be done. But it gave me the confidence and empowerment to start making changes that would eventually lead to a better work-life balance.

Starting my own little rebellion

Rewind to my second school. The marking policy required books to be assessed and marked *at least* every four lessons. This equated in the Humanities to once a fortnight. This resulted in having to mark every night and at weekends to fit it in. In each marking session, staff were required to mark for literacy, identify successes, ask questions and set targets for directed improvement and reflection time.

As previously mentioned, it was taking far too long, so I sought out ways to provide the feedback students needed to progress whilst also ensuring I achieved the school's marking essentials. I tried a variety of strategies and found the most useful to be marking grids.

Marking grids outline the success criteria expected from students and the potential next steps or targets. During an Ofsted visit in summer 2015, my use of marking grids was positively commented on; this gave me the confidence to make further changes to my practice that could hopefully help others.

The positive response from Ofsted on my feedback practice I believe resulted in me being asked to run a Marking and DIRT Workshop for new and current staff during our end of year CPD day.

Without knowing it at the time I used this as an opportunity to start the movement away from marking and instead towards feedback. The workshop aimed to inform new staff on current policy, to improve and support current approaches and to initiate the move to make marking and feedback quicker and more efficient, whilst still providing high-quality feedback to our students. The workshop ended with discussions on how the current marking and DIRT policy could be improved and supported through the use of techniques that I shared, or that others had experienced.

After that I'd regularly discuss and share ideas with colleagues to help them reduce their workload surrounding marking and feedback as well as to seek out further ways to reduce my own. The following academic year I attended Pedagoo Hampshire and presented on 'Less is More: Marking with a Purpose'. The session was popular with standing room only. This was the start of the #FeedbackNOTmarking movement.

Since then I've presented at numerous events on the topic and each time I try to instill a little bit of rebellion in each attendee to go back to their schools and rebel against the systems in place to encourage the move from marking to feedback in all schools.

It's not easy to find the confidence to change things, to take those first steps in standing up or saying no. But without us rebellious teachers, change in our schools will never happen in the way we want it to. Autonomy within schools is vital for teacher happiness, but it needs someone to stand up and fight for that autonomy, to take a stand and seek out change.

Will it be you?

How to be a rebellious teacher

1   Always keep your students in your heart and mind; any change you want to see must directly or indirectly be of benefit to them.

2   Research. Find out what works and what doesn't. We can't refuse to do something because we simply don't want to; evidence is essential to the argument. There must be valid reason.

3   Be passionate about what you believe in. This will support your evidence and argument.

Snippet of insight

"I'd like to say ignore any nonsense school initiatives that don't benefit your students, but that's easy for me to say! It's difficult for newer teachers to be rebels! But I would say that if you work in a school where leadership does not continually strive to minimise workload (for example, by having an efficient centralised detention system) then consider moving to another school. Things may be a lot better elsewhere". *Jo Morgan, Maths Lead Practitioner, Harris Federation and UK Blog Award Winner 2017. Tweets as @mathsjem*

Takeaways

* Leaving teaching completely isn't the only option when you are finding it a challenge.

* There are plenty of options if you're able to be flexible.

* If changing schools, position or hours isn't a possibility, become a rebel teacher. Fight for change in your current setting.

Managing the workload

The workload of a teacher varies in size, diversity and complexity depending on the teachers' career stage, level of responsibility and age of students being taught. There is no doubt however that with all of the juggling of roles and tasks, a teacher's workload can be exhausting, mentally challenging and far too much at times.

However, there are ways to make it work to ensure you have a decent work-life balance. I know because I've managed it (mostly); although there are still numerous crunch points throughout the year when a variety of deadlines seem to amalgamate despite my school's best efforts to disperse deadlines throughout the year, sometimes things just inadvertently overlap. But organisation is key.

Learn to be organised.

This doesn't come naturally to some people; but if you can master being organised, it makes the job a hell of a lot easier. At my second school, upon leaving my year 11 students awarded me with the title 'Little Miss Organised'; that's not to say I don't have moments of chaos, but on the whole, being organised has been one of the most effective ways of reducing stress on a day-to-day basis.

Word of caution: I'm no expert in time management, organisation and productivity; these suggestions are from my experiences, from talking to others and through conducting research to survive up until this point in my career.

Tip 1. Know when you are most productive

We may not be able to plan our day around our personal productivity. Unfortunately those fixed school hours don't change for us. But we can choose whether to work before the school day or after it. Knowing when you are most productive in the day is a helpful aid to getting things done.

For me, on the weekend I'm useless at working after about 11 am. I have too much energy, and my mind dances. Yet if I get up around 7 or 8 am, get working straight away, I can whizz through tasks and jobs. Yet during the week it's a different story. I used to get to work early to crack on with things, but I realised that I'd only get through the tasks that required little thought like printing and photocopying or prepping for the day ahead. Rarely did I have the focus or inclination to mark or plan. It wasn't until my fifth year that I realised I'm most productive between the end of school and 6 pm; after that I'm drained of energy and easily distracted. Since I realised this I've been able plan my time accordingly.

No longer am I in school around 7 am. Instead I enjoy a coffee in the morning and watch the news before making my way to work. I use the efficient period after school to mark and plan. Once my attention dwindles I start to prepare for the next day.

This may not be possible for everyone, particularly those with children or care responsibilities. But even then, you can assess your effectiveness in the time you do have available. Could it be worth getting up slightly earlier or going to bed later if you're more productive?

Everyone's productivity varies. Try working at different times and score your productivity throughout each period on a scale of 0, being unproductive, to 5, being very productive. You may also want to track what you do in this time to assess patterns. From there, organise your time.

If you want to find out more on assessing your productivity, take a look at ultradian cycles or rhythm.

Tip 2. Plan your time

During the first few years I timetabled **everything**, probably a little to excessively. But it helped ease my anxiety surrounding the day and week ahead. Now after experience and learned patience I can plan my time without the need for a variety of timetables plastered over my wall and school planner. Sometimes I even wing it without a to-do list. Crazy or what?!

Timetabling certain activities can be effective at enabling you to maximise the time available.

I really liked Alex Quigley's approach to time which he discusses in 'The Confident Teacher'. He divides time in our working day into *fixed time* and *fluid time*. The *fixed time* he describes as the time that "is largely out of our control". It applies to the core aspects of our jobs which are scheduled into our day, including both our teaching timetable and regular meetings. Whilst *fluid time* "is relatively flexible", this involves the tasks that we have more control over how and when we complete them. These are the things we do on a day-to-day basis other than the actual teaching such as lesson planning, marking and feedback, data input, observing others, communicating with parents, irregular meetings and so on. Alex goes on to suggest we complete a time audit over the course of a week to highlight and focus on the tasks we undertake that can be deemed as fluid and can therefore be timetabled into our *fluid time*.

Once you've identified tasks that require regular attention in your *fluid time*, I'd suggest setting yourself time frames for working before and after school as well as over the weekend.

In the beginning I never set myself time frames, on reflection I wish I had. It meant I wasted time watching TV whilst marking or I'd get distracted by something that wasn't as much of a priority. Nowadays I set myself a time frame for completing tasks and stick to it; I stay at work until 6 pm and take nothing home most days as a result. Although not possible for everyone due to commitments such as family, it's important you don't allow work to consume your life outside of the working day as well.

Next, from your list of tasks, identify your reoccurring weekly priorities. In my first three years these were marking, lesson planning and homework. I'd set up my weekly timetable for these after school and on weekends.

Here's an example. My workplace dictated that books were to be marked every four lessons. Since I taught around fourteen classes, this meant I had to mark a set of books every day including weekends. It was easy to lose track, so I created a fortnightly schedule for marking and assessing books. Next, I worked out which days I had to set and collect homework for each class and would write this into the homework section of the timetable. Finally, I'd create tick boxes to confirm whether books had been marked or not.

After the first year of this, I experimented with different feedback strategies and added a key to the timetable to identify the types of marking and feedback that been undertaken. This helped to determine when it was necessary to carry out a 'deep' marking session. I'll come back to managing the marking, feedback and assessment workload later on in Chapters 6 and 9.

I'd create this timetable at the beginning of each year; it helped me then with organising my remaining *fluid time* around other necessary tasks.

Term 1	Monday	Tuesday	Wednesday	Thursday	Weekend
Classes	Geog – 9Hu2, 9Hu3 9Hu1	Geog – 9Hu2, 9Hu3 11 Geog	11 Geog, 7Hu1 7OM3	8Hu1, 8Hu3 (x2)	Geog - 9Hu1, 9OM1, 8Hu1,7Hu1
Odd Weeks	Year 9 Geog Hu2	Year 9 Geog Hu3	Year 11 Geog (EQ)	Year 8 Hu1	7OM3*
Even Weeks	Year 7 Hu1	9OM1*	Year 11 Geog (EQ)	Year 8 Hu3	Year 9 Geog Hu1
Homework Collect/Set	9Hu2, 9Hu3		Year 11 Geography	8Hu1	9Hu1, 8 Hu3, 7Hu1

Term 6	Week 1	Week 2-	Week 3	Week 4	Week 5	Week 6	Week 7

Bold = Every week if possible *Taught once a week
VF = Verbal Feedback
SA = Self-Assessment
PA = Peer Assessment   DIRT = Directed Improvement and Reflection Time

Figure 4.1 Example of marking and assessment timetable

Tip 3. Task management

Task management is an essential skill to attempt to master early on in your career to save you running into burnout mode later on. I say this because in the past I'd use my PPA time with little consideration of what I wanted to achieve in the time available. Often, I'd do a number of smaller jobs on the to-do that I thought 'needed' doing, only to go and leave the important ones until after school or even worse until I got home, taking up important recharge time. Even with that experience I still find that it is easy to end up wasting PPA time.

In the morning or before leaving the night before, consider your priorities for the day ahead or if you prefer, do it on a Monday morning for the week.

The Eisenhower Matrix is then an effective way to prioritise the tasks on your list based upon their urgency versus their importance. Those that require urgent completion and are highly important you should deal with first, followed by those that are urgent but not so important. If possible consider delegating these tasks. For those that are important but not urgent, give yourself a deadline. Finally, those tasks that are not important or urgent can be left until last, or if no one is chasing you about them they don't need a deadline.

To find out more on the Eisenhower Principle that underpins the matrix visit the Eisenhower website at www.eisenhower.me/eisenhower-matrix/

I like to think that with experience comes the ability to drop things from the to-do list: those tasks that you realise have little to no impact on student outcomes or classroom practice. Which is why it's also important to consider the consequence or impact of each task on your list.

When my to-do list is getting what seems to be uncontrollable, I consider the consequence. If I don't do a task, who will it impact? My students? My colleagues? Just me?

Before adding anything to the to-do list ask yourself these questions

- What's the purpose?

- Who will it benefit?

- Have you been asked to do it?

- Is it vital for student learning or safety?

- Is it going to improve your classroom practice?

Personally, I like to think that if I can't answer yes to at least one of the last two, it probably doesn't need to be done and usually ends up in my not important or urgent list. Never to be completed.

A word of warning on perfectionism

Another thing is don't let perfectionism take over a task. For instance, Twitter is often full of images of work others have created for their students which are beautiful and dazzling. But to what extent do the students need it to look that professional? What benefit will it have on student progress? What influence is there on one's classroom practice?

I'm guilty of it though. I'd set myself tasks that were a result of my own need for perfection, that resulted from an aspiration to produce consistently outstanding lessons, and it wore me down.

This is a realisation that I only achieved after having a breakdown in my fourth year of teaching. So do listen. That resource doesn't need to look like the product of a professional designer that is paid to produce beautiful pieces of work. Use that time to do something urgent or important on the list or even spend that time on doing something for yourself.

Tip 4. Create a template bank

By the time I reached the end of my third year of teaching, I realised that keeping a bank of blank templates on my hard drive was becoming a valuable tool in reducing the time I spent on planning and marking.

Some of the materials I have templates for include:

- My mark book

- PowerPoint format

- Variety of scaffolds (e.g. writing frames, support mats, knowledge organisers etc.)

- Variety of learning activities (e.g. hexagons, card sorts, dominoes, tarsias, heads and tails etc.)

- Marking and feedback grids

- Self or peer assessment sheets

- Vocabulary lists

- Multiple choice quizzes

- Entry/exit tickets

The use of templates has also helped me to simplify my planning. I have a range of go-to learning activities that I regularly apply to the content from which I want my students to learn, thus supporting my efforts to plan backwards.

Tip 5. Plan time for yourself

If you're going to be effective at the job, you must look after yourself. Whilst you timetable and prioritise the workload, never fail to book time in for you. Whether it's a long soak in the bath once a week, a nightly visit to the gym, twenty minutes of reading or whatever else helps you to unwind, get it in the diary. When I searched 'making time for yourself' on google, about 793,000,000 results occurred. I didn't check how many of those are worthwhile and relevant but the variety of sources demonstrate its importance. Everything from the NHS and mental health charities to lifestyle and business magazines recommend it. It's not just teachers that need to look after themselves, but all of us, so encourage your friends and family to participate and make an event of self-care.

There have been a number of studies into the effect of teacher health and wellbeing on student outcomes, and whilst there is limited evidence showing a clear, direct link between the two, there is a clear expectation that such a correlation exists. It is therefore vital that we work to ensure the wellbeing of our students, and by doing so we take the necessary steps to care for our own.

Don't let the teacher guilt stop you from looking after yourself.

Snippets of insight

I posed the question "what advice would you give to help others manage their workload?" to edu-Twitter colleagues. Here's what they have to say:

"Do what is essential first. Have your time for marking and planning, whether it is early morning or after school, and stick to it. Have a shut off time". *Andrew Cowley, Deputy Headteacher and author of 'The Wellbeing Toolkit'. Tweets as @andrew_cowley23*

"Give yourself a working time budget. Adjust what you do to fit in with the time available and don't go over". *Rufus Johnstone, Lead Coach. Tweets as @rufuswilliam*

"Establish routines for yourself – that includes down time. Prioritise, see 'Eat That Frog' by Brian Tracy for time management. Consider having a marking buddy so you keep each other company and commit to get it done. Also share planning and resources. Ask yourself 'Will it Make the Boat Go Faster', see book of same title by Ben Hunt Davies. Basically ask yourself constantly if what you are doing will make a significant difference and if not, don't do it." *Gill Rowland, Senior Lecturer at Canterbury Christ Church University. Tweets as @gillrowland1*

"Focus on the things that make a real difference to your students: master your craft by honing your modelling, explanations and questioning. Spend time where it matters and ask yourself what students are learning from parts of your lesson. If you're not sure it's improving learning then scrap it!" *Rebecca Foster, Head of English. Tweets as @TLPMsF*

"Have an electronic calendar and add all lessons, meetings and other jobs to it and give each task an allotted time to get it done, include personal appointments and requirements too. Add wellbeing, relaxation and family stuff to the same calendar. Manage workload through email messages. Every time you get an email that needs you to do something, add some time to your calendar to get the job done and then file the email. Say no to people as you need to. Work through email messages from oldest to newest, not the opposite. This has worked for me". *Ed Brodhurst, Assistant Headteacher. Tweets as @brodhurst*

"Make lists! Code each item according to when things need to be done by and prioritise using this list. Speak up if you think you are being asked to complete an unreasonable amount of work. One teacher might have more than one head of department if they teach more than one subject, as well as a head of year, all of whom are placing pressures on you and who may not be aware of your workload and what another leader has already asked you to do. However, when speaking to staff about workload, going prepared with a potential solution, makes outcomes easier to achieve". *Sarah Larsen, Teacher of Geography. Tweets as @sarahlarsen74*

"Look at your workload critically. Are you generating additional work yourself? Does everything really need to be laminated? Ask for support if you are struggling. If you are asked to take on additional responsibilities, ask what you can stop doing to make time for them. Focus on what impacts outcomes. If it's not making a difference for the pupils, why are you doing it?" *Sam Collins, Founder of Schoolwell. Tweets at @samschoolstuff*

"If your workload is unmanageable and unsustainable, before you consider leaving that school (or the profession) make it your mission to try and reduce the workload at your school. If the marking burden is too high, suggest more efficient ways of doing it. If planning requirements are ridiculous, look for schemes of work already planned for you. If you have too many meetings, propose to reduce the number. In short, don't feel powerless and act in a powerless way – take some control of the situation. If you face too many obstacles at your school, then find a better school. There are loads of good schools out there that are working hard to reduce teachers' workloads – don't feel your only option is to leave teaching!" *Adrian Bethune, Teacher and author of 'Wellbeing in the Primary Classroom: A Practical Guide to Teaching Happiness'. Tweets as @AdrianBethune*

Takeaways

- Prioritise and plan your time – do the most urgent and important tasks first.

- Plan time for yourself.

- Consider the impact of a task – is it necessary?

- What you can't get done in the time available, you simply can't do.

- Use timetables to stay organised.

- Find shortcuts that work for you.

Surviving

As a teacher at times it can be troublesome juggling and managing the multitude of tasks and responsibilities we encounter within our role. Often, we can be left feeling like we are merely surviving from one day to the next. But it doesn't have to be that way. I know because I've managed to achieve a better work-life balance in recent years, a result that comes from a determination to be proactive, insist on and implement change myself. Although there does need to be amendments in the education system and within our schools, we also need to be mindful of what we can do to manage our time, workload and wellbeing ourselves. This chapter aims to assist you, as new teachers, through the first few years as you learn the art of teaching and develop your classroom practice to enable you to not just survive but thrive.

The following chapter will delve into ways of making our classrooms work for us through careful planning and organisation with suggestions for tried and tested displays that make classroom life easier.

The remainder of this section will explore the problems associated with lesson planning, differentiation, behaviour and marking, whilst providing tried and tested ideas, strategies and solutions to help you to maximise your directed time, manage your workload and improve your wellbeing.

Throughout the section, there will be snippets of insight from a variety of educators along with a range of strategies and examples for you to trial and implement.

5 Setting up your classroom

The classroom. Your space. Your rules. Your domain. The thing about setting up your classroom is that it needs to work for you. Whether you are a primary, secondary or further education teacher, if your fortunate to have a classroom of your own, then your classroom is where you are likely to spend much of your time teaching. You therefore need to make the space your own.

When you set up each year, carefully consider how you can make the classroom space work for you. Consider the layout, expectations, accessibility and displays; can they be positioned and displayed to make it easier for you? Easier for your students?

Layout

Start by assessing the space you have available and how you can best use it to suit your teaching style. Some schools dictate classroom set up, but if you have the freedom to choose, carefully consider how you like your classroom to run.

Will you expect your students to freely access resources and equipment? If so, consider the location of these. Additionally, consider the fact they will become high-traffic areas, keep them easily accessible and free of obstruction. Therefore, you may also want to avoid keeping these away from where you spend much of your time, such as near your desk or the whiteboard to ensure you keep a degree of your own space whilst you work.

If you want students to collaborate as a matter of course, cluster tables into small groups or resource stations. Maybe you frequently hold whole-class discussions then consider a horse-shoe shape. If you prefer to teach from the front rows may be preferable.

Depending on the age range and classroom space, you may desire distinct areas. These areas may include some of the following purposes

- Reading

- Quiet working

- Collaboration

- Multimedia and ICT

- Resource stations

- Individual working

Such areas are more commonly found in primary classrooms yet can help develop independence in later age ranges too; although it can be harder to do due to lack of space.

To counteract the space challenge in the secondary classroom, I like to use flexible seating at times. This involves creating groups of tables for a specific purpose. Students have the flexibility to decide where to sit and can move freely throughout the lesson as they work. Personally, I prefer not to use this consistently as not all activities and lessons support this practice.

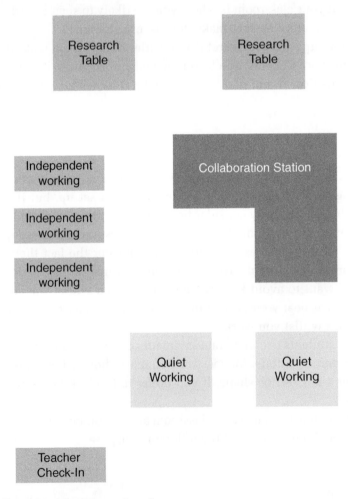

Figure 5.1 Example of flexible seating plan

Remember, though, that you can move your tables any time. Don't be afraid to change your set-up throughout the year to support positive student interactions, accessibility and your teaching style.

Opportunity to think

When setting up your classroom, consider your answers to the following:

- How often do you do group work? Discussions? Paired work? Independent work?

- Do you want students to collaborate as a matter of course or do you prefer students to work independently?

- Which layout best suits the approaches you use most frequently?

- Do you have a preference in the direction students face?

- Do you want students to be able to freely access equipment and resources?

- How will the table layout impact ease of movement around the room?

- Are there areas of the room that will have higher levels of traffic than others?

  Consider the ease of movement and limiting distraction of other students.

Rules and expectations

When setting up your classroom, consider your rules and expectations for students.

In my NQT year, rules and expectation sheets were placed on every window of my portacabin classroom. I realized that this was excessive; one or two would have sufficed. Carefully consider where to place rules and expectation posters. You may find yourself referring to these during the school year if you need to remind students; I recommend either having them near your board, at the back of the room or near the door. Somewhere you can easily draw attention to them.

If you're going to create a reward system, consider where you will locate this early on. Make it distinguishable and easy to access for both teachers and students. Again, ideally locate it somewhere that is easy to draw attention to.

Ensure students understand your classroom rules and expectation from day one of teaching them. It will require repetition and at times you will feel like a nag, but consistency in your message is key.

Equipment and resources

It's not for everyone, but I like to give free access to equipment and resources that students may require during lessons such as glue, scissors, rulers and textbooks along with scaffolding, challenge and extension activities. Therefore, I keep these all easily accessible for students on window sills and display boards. On the other hand, I do have a cupboard in which I keep resources and equipment that I don't want students to freely help themselves too such as pencils and pens as all too often these go missing.

Carefully consider the equipment and resources you'd like students to have access to and where you can locate these for easy access and limited disruption. Window sills are often useful as are the tops of shelving units. You may also wish to consider if you will have a lending system in place for equipment.

In my first school I created an in/out board for borrowing essentials. Students were issued with uniform cards at the start of the year by the pastoral team. If students weren't dressed appropriately or had failed to bring essential equipment, the card would be signed by the member of staff. After five signatures a detention would be set. I decided to make use of these cards. If a student borrowed any of the essential equipment they handed their card in and could take out the necessary equipment from the board. When they returned the equipment, they took their card back. I used the cards to my advantage at times to build relationships; for instance, particularly with challenging classes, I would not sign their uniform cards providing they returned the equipment in perfect condition. This 'give and take' deal helped with the behaviour management of these classes.

In another school, I numbered all my pens, pencils and rulers. Students would write their initials on the board and the number of the item they borrowed. With the classes that weren't quite so trustworthy, they'd have to hand in an item of personal importance such as their rucksack, phone or watch. On return of my equipment, they'd get their possession back. I always found it highly entertaining when a student would realise and come rushing back to my room out of breath to return my equipment and collect their own.

Opportunity to think

- What equipment and resources will you want students to freely access?
- Where can these be easily accessed in your room?
- Will you have a lending system?
- Will there be any consequences for borrowing essential equipment?

Creating displays

In my NQT year I filled my portacabin classroom with rules and procedure posters; they weren't looked at by the students. I rarely referred to them. They were a waste of paper and more so my time. I had used this little display space for displaying student work, merely for the attractiveness of it. When I changed schools, I had a fresh canvas and thus decided to think about how the displays could truly benefit my students. I went through several display approaches before I found what worked best for me and my students.

Opportunity to think

- How often do you or want to refer to what's on your walls?

- How often do you or want to encourage students to look at the work on the walls?

- How often do you get students to engage with the displays?

- Are you encouraging students to create work for display. If so, with what purpose?

Displays – purpose and uses

In many school's displays are an expectation. Some schools even have a list of non-negotiables for what **must** be on display. Yet creating displays can take time to design, produce and maintain. Time that could otherwise be used for planning, marking, assessment . . . and so on.

Before creating any display consider the time it will take to create it versus the impact it will have on your classroom practice or student outcomes. Consider these questions before getting started:

1   What is the purpose of the display?

2   Will the display contribute to future learning?

3   Will the display invite active involvement or be a passive exhibition of information?

Let's look at each one in turn

Purpose – what exactly do you want students to take away from the display? A display's purpose can range from providing key vocabulary for the subject or topic of study to hints, tips and model answers, from tasks to extend, challenge and reflect upon or to sharing success criteria such as GCSE grade descriptors.

Contribution – How will it contribute to students' current and future learning? A display's purpose needs to be of benefit to the learner and should contribute to their future learning in some way. Contribution to learning can be as simple as the display serving as a reminder of prior learning to highlight previous content covered for students to draw upon or the key vocabulary for the present topic of study with new words added as they are covered. The key is for contribution to learning to continue over time. However, this needs regular referral to the displays to remind students of the content they hold and to refrain from them becoming passive exhibits of information.

Active involvement – Displays that just sit there to present information, that require no input from the student and is merely there to make the room look nice are a waste of time and space. The best displays encourage active engagement from students. For instance, if you are displaying student work, engage students by incorporating their comments on the work by creating what a good one looks like (WAGOLL) for students to compare their own work against it or create a generic checklist of success criteria so that students can assess each piece of work they do. Those that achieve all aspects of the criteria can go on display as a model for others.

Frequency of change – At the start of the year, consider whether the display can be static, adapted or completely changed throughout the year. I find that displays that provide a purpose throughout the year are most useful and least time consuming. Once set up they are ready for the academic year ahead with just a few amendments over time. Using things like magazine holders and wallet folders are extremely useful; staple them to the notice board and replace the content as and when required.

In my current classroom I have just five displays, three of which are static displays and don't change throughout the year, whilst the other two are amended as and when necessary. Each display has its own purpose and contribution to my students' learning experience.

1   Finished board for early finishers – when a student has finished, reviewed their work and if their work has been peer-assessed, they choose an activity from the three options: extend, assess or reflect. Each activity is generic and encourages the relevant action.

2   Help Yourself board – this board contains a range of generic scaffolding and support materials that students are either directed to or can help themselves to as and when they need the necessary support. In addition, it holds folders for the three GCSE Geography papers, each containing scaffolding and revision materials for students to freely access.

3   ACE discussion and peer-assessment routines – this board simply outlines the actions for ACE (accept, challenge or extend) discussions and the routine for ACE peer assessment.

4   Geography Gems – a set of hints and tips for success in geography applicable for Key Stage 3, 4 and 5.

5   Student work – I have a washing line between two display boards; the work is changed every term to give students examples of work from previous year groups and for current students to inspire students when they complete their own versions.

Avoid clutter

Have you ever entered a classroom and not known where to look due to the sheer amount of display material? I know I have. Research shows that a cluttered classroom can have a detrimental impact on learning; there's a fine line between the appropriate level of stimulation and over-stimulation (Fisher et al., 2014; Barrett et al., 2015)

Ideally classroom layout and display space should be sufficiently stimulating but with a degree of order, control and calm-colouring to reduce potential over-stimulation of students, particularly younger students or those with ASD. Too much colour, clutter and change to the classroom environment can have detrimental impacts on learning progress by encouraging more time off task.

To create an effective classroom environment to support learning consider the following for your display space

- Keep it organised and clearly laid out.

- Use calm colouring.

- Avoid patterns. Instead use blocks of colour

- Avoid stimulating display material around the main point of visual attention such as the whiteboard.

However, it's ideal to also avoid under-stimulation as well; research also indicates that bare classrooms can potentially have an impact on learning outcomes and student progress.

Displays that work for you

Personally, I've come to find that displays that work best are those I can refer to on a regular basis. It's all well and good having beautiful displays of student work or ideas and resources but if you're not going to refer students to them, then why bother?

As previously mentioned, consider carefully how you might make use of the display space in your room: the purpose, contribution to learning and whether you want students to have active involvement in them.

The following are possible approaches to creating displays that work for you.

Speak like a 'insert subject specialist'

I first saw this idea over on Twitter as Speak like a Geographer by Kate Stockings (tweets as @geography_kes). The idea is simple: the display provides students with subject-specific terminology by offering alternatives to words they may regularly use. It can be static display or change with the topic of study with clear application for both primary and secondary. If you can't afford to give an entire display board to this, why not turn it into support sheets students can collect and use?

Working walls

Working walls are a public display of the learning process. This means that they evolve each day and/or lesson. Many primary schools I've come across have working walls; yet very few secondary schools implement such an approach. However, they can be an effective way of demonstrating the learning process to students. Why not try them out by using them for planning the approach to a task, inquiry or investigation? Maybe start a topic with students asking questions, follow up with students researching the topic and add it to the board before ending with students answering the questions. Alternatively, provide a topic-related picture or photo in the centre and get the students to question the image and its relationship to the topic. As students progress through the topic, they add what they've learnt to the display along with research and other stimulants before finally using what they've learnt to complete a set task or assessment.

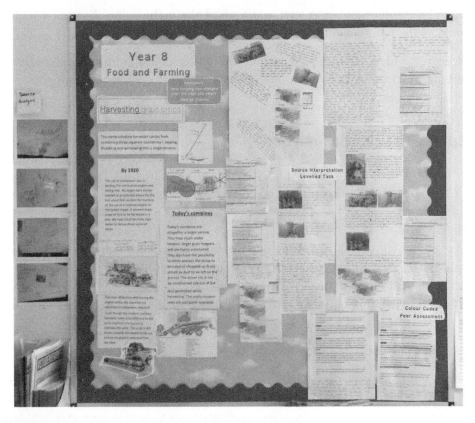

Figure 5.2 Example of a working wall, includes self-directed homework, classwork and assessed pieces of extended writing

With a working wall, as learners progress through a unit of work, ideas, examples and topical stimulants are added to the board to support them in their learning journey. To keep the working wall effective, it's vital to have a clear layout to avoid a monster of mess building up, thus reducing the impact of the display.

Finished board

Ever have those moments when students have finished, have self- or peer-assessed, have reviewed their work and exceeded your time frame expectations? What do you do then?

A finished board provides activities to encourage students to extend their learning or to encourage students to assess and reflect on their learning and progress through a wide variety of generic activities. I first discovered the idea from Kerry Madrick (@misstait_85) after seeing her version in the online publication UKEd Chat Magazine. Kerry has also kindly made all of her resources available for you to download from her blog (https://misstait.wordpress.com/2014/08/29/finished/).

Similar can be done with generic activities to stretch and challenge students.

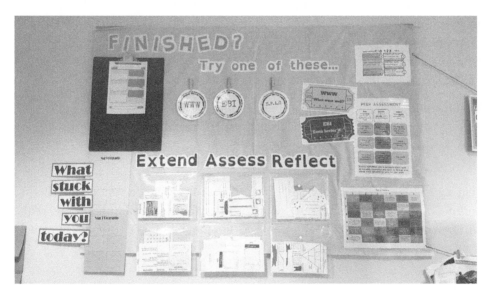

Figure 5.3 Example of a 'Finished . . . try one of these' board

Repeated errors

Once you've been teaching a few years, you start to notice the same or similar errors or misconceptions occur each year. The repeated errors board aims to limit these before they arise. Use this display to identify to students the errors or misunderstandings students regularly have and how to correct them. In geography, identifying Africa as a country rather than a continent is probably one of the biggest repeated errors. It would certainly be my first to go on this kind of display. What would you put onto yours?

Key content

Whether for a topic or whole subject, this display provides the key content students require for their work. It's kind of like a knowledge organiser blown up onto a display board. Provide students with the key content of the topic or subject such as terminology, dates, processes, formulas and so on. For science class, this may be key terminology, processes, investigation stages and formulas relevant to the current topic of study. Whereas history may include the names of key people, important dates and events along with snippets of information to remind students of the cause and consequence of each.

Metacognition

Why not make use of a display board or resource station to promote extension, assessment and reflection on the learning process to help students understand their cognitive process in learning. A metacognition board could divide tasks into the same three categories as used in my finish board; extend, assess and reflect. It should get students to 'think about thinking'.

Other possible display ideas to make displays work for you:

Exam technique – strategies to help with exams
Exam structure – an outline of the exam structures and command words
Revision boards – resources to support revision
Keyword stations – lists of keywords students can take away

What a good one looks like (WAGOLL) and what a bad one looks like (WABOLL) – examples of work that mean success criteria and examples that require improvement. With the latter either create them yourself or ensure you ask permission from students.

Resource stations

A resource station is an area of the room with resources for a defined purpose. No matter the age range you are teaching, resource stations are helpful tools for developing independent learners. Resource stations can have a variety of purposes from self-marking to research, for scaffolding or to challenge. They can be a permanent feature of the classroom or temporary. The following are suggested uses of the resource station.

Research

If you are fortunate to have access to technology in your room, whether it be a PC or tablet device or two, consider making use of the technology for students to carry out research and to find answers for themselves. If you're not lucky enough to have the technology, consider putting useful books and resources into the research station for students to browse.

Marking and assessment

Resource stations with this focus require some pre-set up. Students will require mark schemes and answers for the work they have produced. This is much easier for subjects such as mathematics where there are correct answers, whereas in subjects such as English or geography require some teacher input. Therefore, in advance of being able to self-mark students also require structured support to enable them to develop the skills required to mark and assess their own work. I start teaching self and peer assessment with my classes from day one. We may start with a simple tick, flick and correct but within a few weeks we move onto a more strategic approach.

Once you have routines for self and peer assessment, teach students how to use mark schemes. As students start to develop their understanding and assessment skills, you can slowly step back and allow students to select the materials from the station to allow them to self and/or peer assess independently. If you do this well enough by the end of the year, students will be assessing most of their own work in class, allowing you to check, correct and challenge students more.

Self-help

For a self-help station to work, resources and facilities are provided for students to find answers for themselves or to seek help from others. Resources such as knowledge organisers, fact files and textbooks may be provided along with ICT facilities if available. You may decide to nominate a student as the student support for the day, lesson or topic dependent on the subject being taught and the ability of students; they can help others to find answers when they need a little support.

Scaffolding

I have discovered that stations that allow students to choose their own scaffolding are extremely useful. The station consists of a variety of general resources to support students in a variety of tasks such as sentence starter mats, synonym mats, laminated note-taking sheets, timeline sheets, keyword lists, structure strips and so on.

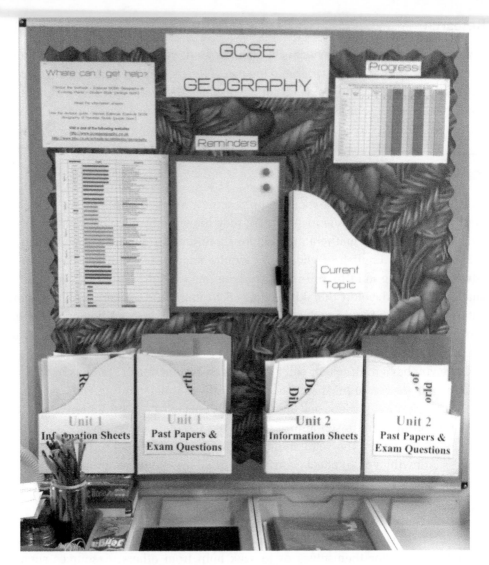

Figure 5.4 Example of a self-help station for GCSE students

Initially I give scaffolds to students, then as they become more independent I remove them. After several uses and experience of how to use, if students are struggling with an activity or task, they can help themselves to scaffold resources that would help them. It takes time and students will require some suggestion to make use of the resources before developing the confidence to decide for themselves as to whether they need it or not. But I've generally found that students are more likely to make use of these resources if they have decided for themselves that they wish to use them. However, I can't say this will be the case for everyone.

Challenge and extend

Although work should be challenging to start with, sometimes students do exceed expectations. Therefore, perhaps you have go-to strategies to challenge and extend students beyond the work that you've originally set? If so, keep templates at a resource station. You can then encourage students to 'level up' if they feel the original task was too easy for them or to extend on their completed work. If you need inspiration check out these websites:

www.missbsresources.com/teaching-and-learning/stretching-the-challenge
http://mikegershon.com/resources/

And for the vagabonds . . .

If you're not lucky enough to have a room of your own, or perhaps you share with a part-time member of staff or simply don't have a fixed room, then many of these strategies can be harder to achieve but not impossible. You'll just need a trolley or a similar device to store and transport your resources.

In the trolley keep all your essentials such as stationery and equipment along with folders with your daily resources. To create stations, print the resources and store them in expanding folders. Make a label to identify the content of each and put them out at the start of lesson. Give students the responsibility for the content and for ensuring that all resources are returned to the folder before the end of the lesson by including a content checklist. Additionally, although you may not have display space you can still make use of display ideas, create the resources and pop them in a display book for students to access. If you can get a hold of the ones that prop themselves up even better.

Taking time to set up

We all have our preferences. But if you can get as much of the classroom set up in advance of the first day of school, do it. Usually, the first day or two of the school year is given over to staff training, and although we'd like to have time on those days to set up, it's often unlikely that you will. This doesn't mean you have to spend all summer preparing for the year ahead.

If you get gained time in the summer term, use some of this time for preparation. If not, choose just a day or two in the holidays (or more if you prefer) and limit yourself to that. What's not done over those days can be done in the new school year. You can even get students to help.

One rule that I'd recommend for the beginning of the year preparations is to make sure your room is laid out and equipped how you want it to be. Displays and stations can wait, but having your room set up with the basics means that routines and procedures are set up from day one.

Keeping up appearances

I've now used my finished board resources for four years at two schools, and they're still going strong. Every now and then I'll add resources to the array already there, but I've not had to throw any out. Preferably try to use tear-proof paper, as it's better for the environment than laminating. But if you have to, laminate the classroom resources you'd like to maintain.

In summary, make your room your own. Allow it to reflect you, your values and ethos. But also make it work for you. Dedicating time to careful planning, organisation and classroom set up does pay off, and although initially time consuming, once you've created a foundation of classroom resources, if maintained, they save time elsewhere in the year.

Takeaways

- Plan your classroom so that it is functional for you.

- Carefully consider the layout and organisation of the room; consider the high-traffic areas and how to reduce distractions.

- Do you want students to have free access to equipment and resources. If so, where will you place them?

- Displays can do a job. Consider the role and purpose of each display versus the time taken to create and renew. Is it necessary or purposeful?

- Avoid clutter where possible as it can have an impact on learning.

- Interactive displays and resource stations are an effective way to help learners to become more independent in the learning process.

References

Barrett, P., Davis F., Zhang, Y., & Barrett, L.(2015) The Impact of Classroom Design on Pupils' Learning: Final Results of a Holistic, Multi-Level Analysis. *Building and Environment*, 89, 118–133.

Fisher, A. V., Godwin, K. E., & Seltman, H. (2014) Visual Environment, Attention Allocation, and Learning in Young Children: When Too Much of a Good Thing May Be Bad. *Psychological Science*, 25(7), 1362–1370.

6 Lesson planning

Planning lessons is probably one of my favourite parts of being a teacher. Although this may not be the case for everyone, I do know quite a few people that would agree. Whilst enjoyable, lesson planning can be challenging; there is a huge amount to think about for every lesson, series of lessons and unit of work.

Imagine one lesson being a one-hour presentation to business colleagues. You'd plan the outcome, what you want staff to take away from it. You'd consider the name of the presentation to identify to staff the purpose. You'd put the information on slides that you want to share with them. You might have a small task or two that you want staff to do there and then. You might also have a task you want staff to go away and do to implement the information you've shared with them.

Sounds easy right?

But for teachers it's far more than that.

Firstly, we don't just plan one of these presentations. There will be several over the course of the day. Secondly, in a business scenario you're likely to have several hours during the working week to produce this presentation. Thirdly, there is much more to your presentation that you have to consider. It's not just about disseminating that information from you to them. You must consider how to engage your audience for the length of time, whether you need to differentiate or scaffold so that everyone in the audience can access the presentation. You must demonstrate that your audience has made progress from the start to the end of your presentation by assessing how well they have interacted with it and whether they have taken away from the presentation what you wanted them to take away. Finally, you will have to assess whether they've remembered what you presented to them today at a later date. Can they recall your presentation and the subsequent presentations? Can they apply their understanding of each presentation?

Now does that really sound easy?

Oh wait, I've forgotten to add that you'll spend much of the time planning the presentation outside of the working day along with the assessment of how well the audience progressed and engaged. Additionally, you'll need to provide feedback to the audience on both the work they completed during the presentation and the task they were set to complete afterwards, followed by requiring them to act on that feedback to close any gaps in their understanding. All whilst potentially being observed and judged.

Now it's starting to sound quite challenging and rather time consuming right?

Let's not forget that you will also need to consider all the other aspects of the role such a pastoral care, reporting, communications, parent's evenings, open evenings . . . the list goes on. Being a teacher is far more than planning and teaching lessons.

If all those considerations weren't enough there are also the myths that influence how we plan and teach. In some cases, the myths influence how schools dictate to staff how lessons ought to be planned and taught. In other cases the myths simply influence our independent planning and aspirations. I decided to find out from teachers some of the reoccurring myths they have experienced and address them.

But before we start looking at some of the myths offered, the biggest and most important myth to address in my opinion is the concept of being an 'outstanding' teacher.

I'm not a fan of this term. Sometimes it's used positively to praise and reward, and other times its used discriminatively to embarrass others, both those deemed outstanding and those not yet there. My advice is. . .

Forget trying to be outstanding; you don't need that label

Once upon a time, perhaps 'outstanding' could be measured by ticking off a list of success criteria that you could perform on the day of observation and achieve the judgement by making sure you did everything on that list. But did ticking off success criteria really make for an outstanding teacher? Would outstanding in one school equate to outstanding in another? What does an outstanding teacher really look like? Everyone's outstanding is different.

Then there's the health implications of being 'outstanding' that concern me. If you try to be 'outstanding' 100% of the time, trust me, it will result in burnout. But if you're consistently good and thus demonstrating high-quality teaching and good standards of practice that inspires, challenges and promotes positive learning, then that makes you an outstanding teacher. You don't need the label to be effective. Remember that: consistently good is good enough.

Common myths

"Teacher training adequately prepares you to plan lessons", Amy Wheatley, Key Stage 5 History Teacher. Tweets as @Miss_Whee

Initial teacher training can only teach you so much in a year. Although we're taught the basics of lesson planning, we develop our practice over the training year and hopefully we feel relatively confident in our abilities by the end of it. There is so much more to learn than what we take away from ITT. Learning to teach effectively is a long-term process; there's just not enough time in the teacher training process to cover everything.

Amy, who is from an FE background, went on to mention that during her ITT year no one explicitly told her that lesson planning isn't just what you're teaching, but HOW you're going to teach it. After training she found that when faced with a blank lesson plan, she struggled to apply what she'd learnt in training to how she envisaged the lesson.

Others that I've spoken to agree, whilst some have also said the opposite: they were taught to think about how they will teach the students rather than what they will be teaching the students. They were encouraged to use card sorts, group work, discussion and debates, the list goes on, but what were the students truly taking away from the lesson?

We need a mixture of both to be truly effective, and we need to think about learning over a bigger time frame than each individual lesson. Thus rather than plan forward, we ought to be planning backwards.

Before you start lesson planning, identify exactly what you want students to take away, the skills and the knowledge over the course of the topic or unit. Then, consider how you will broach this. How will they gain that knowledge? How will they develop or apply those skills? What will they take away from individual lessons? How will this build up the big picture? And finally, how will you know they have learnt what you wanted them to learn?

Essentially this means that we need to stop trying to make lessons all engaging and exciting; we need to think about the basics, about the big picture. What do you want students to learn? How are they going to learn it? Then you can start lesson planning.

"After the first year it's easy because you've already got everything planned!!" Bethan White, History Teacher. Tweets as @beasle95

Teaching doesn't become easy, but it does get easier with experience. Whilst you may have the resources for the following year, as classes change meaning we need to cater for this. Our practice develops, and we will want to adapt our approaches to suit our new students. We may come across new ideas and inspiration. We may want to incorporate these. Curriculums change; lessons and resources must keep up. Teaching is a dynamic and ever-changing world, and we can't just churn out the same lessons year after year. But we can adapt what we have, avoid starting from scratch where possible and collaborate with others to reduce the impact of potential changes.

"It takes twice as long to plan a lesson well as it does to teach it" Kate Sawyer, primary school teacher. Tweets as @Dorastar1

If you have routines, go-to strategies and a strong understanding of your subject, this should not be the case. A well-planned lesson can take just a few minutes to plan whilst a poorly planned lesson, despite the time and effort, can take hours to create. It's about understanding the pedagogy and purpose of what you choose to do along with knowing the outcomes you expect to achieve that creates a good lesson, not the time it takes to plan and prepare.

In Jim Smith's book, *The Really Lazy Teacher's Handbook* (2017) he advocates that students should be working harder than the teacher. The book offers a wide variety of strategies to produce highly effective lessons without the burdensome preparation and planning; I highly recommend reading it.

"You can just download all lesson plans and resources you need off the internet". Becky Mogg, Drama and English Teacher

Simply, no matter how good you are at searching the internet, this one simply is not true.

Numerous times I've started with "oh I'll just quickly look to see if there is anything on" . . . and before I know it I'm down a rabbit hole that takes me further and further away from what I'd started out looking for. Sometimes you can spend more time looking for something readymade than if you were to just start from scratch with that resource. I know I won't be the only one to have done it.

If you can't find what you are looking for within ten minutes, give up. Don't waste any more time trying to find it. Instead I'd suggest one of two routes. If it's not something you need immediately, put a shout out on Twitter or on an education-based Facebook group; often someone has what you will be looking for or a point to start from. The second option: just make it yourself.

And when I say make it yourself, that doesn't mean you need to spend hours making a beautiful resource. Basic is perfect, although admittedly it took me a few years to realise this.

"They have to write something down in their books every lesson" Annon

In the UK, Ofsted do not expect to see work in books every lesson. Therefore schools shouldn't either.

For some learning, it may not be necessary for students to have the information in their books. If for example you're teaching exam classes, then it's more important that they then take what they learnt and apply it in a way that means the student has access to the information for revision at a later date, but still it doesn't mean they need to write everything down every lesson. Allow students to explore the learning taking place.

I've often found that if students are not writing in their books, they tend to be more creative and take risks with their learning. They tend not to mind making mistakes as if it's not a part of their book, it can be disposed of. They don't have to commit as much.

One of my favourite techniques is allowing students to write on the tables with whiteboard pens. At first students are reluctant, but once they get into it they splurge with what they write. I think it's the confidence in knowing that it can easily be removed, they don't have to commit to it. In fact, in the past I had a student that hated writing, his book was empty of content. Yet when I allowed him to write on the table, he wrote more than I'd ever seen him write. Instead of making him copy it into his book, I'd then take a photo and print it and glue it in.

Writing on tables is cheap and easy, but ensure you set clear rules, outline expectations and have plenty of cloths and cleaning spray on hand.

If you're concerned about evidencing work students do outside of their books, then you can take photos or scan work before printing and gluing it in. Alternatively, if you have access to a tablet or students can use their own devices you could consider using apps such as Seesaw and ClassDojo to allow students to keep digital portfolios of their work.

"A lesson must always comprise 3 parts: starter, main activity, plenary", Anon

This was exactly how I was taught during my PGCE and subsequently into my NQT year. It still haunts my planning to this day and although I still use this as the basis for planning learning, it doesn't control my lesson structure anymore.

I remember wasting time thinking of the perfect starter and plenary tasks. Activities to engage my students in the first 5 minutes as they arrived in dribs and drabs and exciting plenaries that made students consider what they learnt that lesson, yet which had no later application. It took a few years to accept that you can end a lesson without a plenary and you can start a lesson without a starter. Guess what, the world doesn't implode.

The guidance on lesson structure and format changes and varies with time; some schools even insist on specific approaches, yet Ofsted do not expect to see any specific structure or lesson format. Lessons can take any shape or format providing it leads to positive outcomes for students. The routine you create maybe pre-determined by your school but don't let that control your lessons too much; if you're being observed perform to the required format but if you're not don't let it govern what you do in the classroom. Do what works for you and your students.

"A written lesson plan must be detailed and carefully followed to produce a good lesson" Natalie Snuggs, SEN primary and secondary teacher

Written lesson plans do not need to be incredibly detailed. They do not need to have what students will be doing at the same time as what the teacher will be doing. They do not need to account for every second of the lesson. A written lesson plan can be brief and still be robust.

You see, a detailed lesson plan does not make a good lesson, it is the point of delivery that makes it. If you spend no time at all planning a lesson including the resources, differentiation etc, it probably won't be particularly successful. Yet if you spend too long planning, pouring your heart and soul into it, you may not achieve what you set out to and be left feeling disappointed. There's a fine line between too little planning and too much planning. As you develop, this balance changes. You can spend less time planning and still produce highly effective lessons, especially as you develop a toolkit of effective strategies.

Additionally, it's okay if a lesson doesn't go to plan. It's perfectly acceptable for students not to get out of the lesson what you anticipated, it's fine for a task to not go the way you planned and if they didn't get through the anticipated content. What's important is that you reflect and amend your planning; it's your response that matters.

For instance, I used to beat myself up (metaphorically) if a lesson didn't go as planned. For several years, I was under the impression that I had to rigidly follow the lesson I'd created. Not just that but planning had to be sufficiently detailed to allow another teacher to teach the planned lesson. Turned out neither were true.

I planned meticulously for observations, so much so that I could guarantee that a non-specialist observer could teach the lesson from the lesson plans I'd submit. My training had taught me to do it this way. When I continued this into my NQT I was praised for my planning, and so I continued to do so. I even over-planned a five-minute lesson plan. That was until I became Head of Department and saw that others did not plan this meticulously and still produced highly effective lessons.

Yet some of my best lessons have been those whereby I've gone completely off plan. The students didn't learn what I intended but learnt so much more. Sometimes, you also just have to go with the flow. Be flexible and take diversions in the learning process.

So, remember this, lesson plans are a plan. They can be minimal and still be robust. They are not definitive. They should be flexible and adaptable, like learning. If you don't make it through everything in the planned lesson, carry it over or adapt homework to allow for completion. Don't feel fixed in your lesson planning. Allow it to flow and amend it to what takes place in the class. Stretch those that need it and support those that struggle.

"You have to use technology if you want to be outstanding", Marissa Tomkins, Curriculum Leader of MFL. Tweets as @marissa_tomkins

All too often technology is used to dazzle and engage students with minimal impact on learning; it requires effective preparation, a strong understanding of its use and a skilful application to get the true benefits of it. Yet all too often technology can be lauded as a tool to transform our teaching without the training to support us to do so.

For example, in my second school, teachers were provided with an iPad. I had no idea how to use it and never received any training on how to use it. I taught myself and used a variety of tools and apps that allowed me to take photos of students work, annotate it and print it off. In the classroom, I rarely used it beyond that simply because I didn't know how to.

Technology can be an effective tool for teaching, but it shouldn't be used to replace well researched and documented pedagogy. Technology has a time and place in the classroom; don't feel like you have to use it every lesson, term or topic. Carefully select when and where it would be appropriate; don't just use it to dazzle an observer or to engage the inattentive students if it doesn't add any real value to the lesson.

Lesson planning is time consuming. It requires skill and mastery as well as one's continual learning to be truly effective. But there is one thing I've learnt to do, but only after several years in teaching, is to question what I'm told, to consider its impact and to look for evidence before implementing. Since usually you can trust your instinct, if it adds work to your to-do list, increases stress and has no evidence to support it, it's not worthwhile. So before implementing new regimes, question its relevance and purpose and perhaps ask leaders to what extent it will benefit classroom practice or improve student outcomes. If no-one can answer this sufficiently, be that rebel teacher.

Reducing the workload

When I first started teaching I worked hard to make my lessons engaging, whizzy and full of variety. Despite having a three-part lesson, each lesson was very different to the last. During my PGCE and NQT year I'd plan lessons by looking at the SoW and planning each lesson by what the scheme said should be taught. I realise now that it made teaching rigid and meant that I was pretty much teaching to the test at the end of the topic.

It wasn't until about half way through my NQT year that I started to see that good pedagogy is not so much about planning lesson by lesson but about planning learning over time.

When I became Head of Humanities I was provided with the opportunity to start from scratch. The school was in its first year of opening. The former Head of Department left nothing behind so I literally had a blank canvas to work with. Whilst at times it was hard, it meant I learnt a lot about structuring learning over time. For each topic for each year group I'd consider the knowledge and understanding required, identify the skills I needed for them to develop, and would create a variety of forms of summative assessment and organise opportunities for formative assessment. It was only then that I began to really understand long-term planning, learning and assessment.

With the essentials above, how exactly have I managed to reduce my workload surrounding lesson planning? Firstly, it has taken time, research and practice. Don't expect to be able to do so immediately; be patient. Collaborate with other members of staff, schools and teachers elsewhere. Share resources, ideas and inspiration to reduce how frequently your starting from scratch. Then consider these five steps.

1   Plan for progress.

2   Simplify it.

3   Embrace routine.

4   Plan for feedback.

5   Scaffold and model.

I Plan for progress

I'm completely guilty of it, planning the process and not the progress. Many a time in the past I've found a resource or activity I liked and planned around it, finding a way to make it fit my scheme of work or lesson objectives. Other times I've started my planning process by considering how I'm going to get my students to learn what I want them to learn rather how they will progress from their starting point over time. I'm sure I'm not the only one guilty of it. However, as I gained experience I started to look more at the bigger picture and plan for progress over time.

In *Mark, Plan, Teach*, Ross Morrison McGill discusses how lesson planning is a cognitive process that requires us to think about the bigger picture and not just about the lesson we are planning. He goes on to explore how teachers have a tendency to either plan by activity, plan by coverage or over plan completely. So how can we move away from lesson planning and more towards this planning for progress?

Plan backwards. Keep reading for more information on this.

2 Simplify it

Primary teachers imagine this; it's last thing on a Friday, and your class is wild, excitable and annoying each other but you still need to teach them history. You plan an array of activities to keep them engaged. They spend just five minutes on each one, and you hope they will take away that snippet of knowledge you've intended the activity to give them.

Secondary teachers, imagine this; it's last thing on Friday you have 'that class'. You want to make them enjoy the lesson, so they work hard and learn what they need to learn. You plan an array of activities to keep them on their toes. They bounce around completing one after another until they have had a go at all of them.

But from both scenarios, what have they taken away? The ability to think quickly? The ability to complete the activity within the time frame set? Have they even learnt what you wanted them to learn? Did you spend hours planning the lesson? Did it even go to plan?

Been there, done that.

In recent years, I've learnt to simplify how I teach. Rather than trying to include a range of activities, resources and student choice I now opt for one learning activity which develops through the lesson or through a series of lessons. Not all students will start at the same point, dependent on their individual competencies, and not all students will reach the same outcome by the end of the activity. But all of them will progress, be challenged and experience success.

To do this start by considering the end-point; what do you want your students to know and be able to do by the end of the lesson, the series of lessons, the topic, the term or even the school year? Yes, you'll need think big and work backwards.

Then plan how you will get your students there.

In *Teaching Backwards*, Andy Griffith and Mark Burns discuss how 'teaching backwards is a journey that starts with the end clearly in mind'. It is the learning intention that gives the learning journey its "shape, direction and structure". To plan for progress, you need to know where you are going, then plan the small steps of how you'll get there. This approach has had one of the biggest impacts on my lesson planning as it views learning as a journey with the destination always in mind. It has helped me to organise assessment, marking, feedback and process and by doing so reduce my workload.

Additionally, simplify the range of activities that you use and use them regularly. Student's will become adept at the approach and can then spend longer on developing their thinking and understanding as opposed to trying to understand what the task entails. I used to try all sorts of activities. There was a lack of consistency and thus greater input from me each lesson to explain what they had to do. It also meant students could use the excuse "I don't understand what I'm meant to be doing" far too often for my liking.

In Jim Smith's *The Really Lazy Teacher's Handbook*, he describes a principle entitled 'reduce, reuse, recycle' for simplifying lesson planning. The idea being that we 'reduce' the range of pedagogical practices we use and 'reuse' those what we find to be effective, which then are to be 'recycled' to different classes, subjects and years groups. This strategy then means that students become aware of and "learn the behaviours, practices and outcomes associated with each approach" (Smith, 2017).

I like this strategy of limiting the range of pedagogical practices, and by using a select range of tasks, I've been able to create a routine that gets students working and engaged sooner rather than later. That doesn't mean I don't try out new and exciting ideas, I'm just more selective about it and consider the benefit to learning that the activity will bring before investing time into implementation.

3 Embrace routine

Consider developing a routine for your lessons. For instance start the lesson with a recap, students learn new content and apply it before ending the lesson with a review and reflection. Do what works for you and your students. Some schools insist on a defined lesson routine; whilst you may have to follow the set routine, you can make it your own.

Since it is so engrained in me from training, I still pretty much use a three-part lesson routine – a starter task to review or introduce content, the main body of learning with assessment for learning embedded and a plenary which supports and promotes reflection and metacognition.

A word of caution

Throughout my PGCE and NQT years, I worked with the three-part lesson and I was strict at sticking to it, which left me disappointed at times when I didn't get through everything I planned. Since then I've learnt that this approach to lessons isn't always a productive use of time. Sometimes students just need those last few minutes to complete a task to the best of their ability. Instead I'd suggest creating a finished board, marking station or editing stations which enable students to move on in their own time for those times when you don't feel the plenary or reflection is worthwhile.

If you embrace a routine, don't feel like you have to maintain these routines for individual lessons. The routine can be a process you use for, or instead of, a series of lessons.

For example, my year 8's at present study a unit on Sustainability and China. They spend several lessons learning about aspects of life in China: the physical geography, industrial development, demographic change and pollution. Those lessons follow a routine; after students complete a relevant starter task, the main learning then occurs followed by some sort of reflection. Once they've done the initial inquiry lessons, they then complete an assessed piece of work which gets them evaluating how sustainable China is. To do this they write a National Geographic style article over a series of three or four lessons.

The lesson routine changes to become an ongoing routine for the series of lessons spent on the task.

■ During the first lesson we recap everything we've covered in previous lessons, then students plan their articles. Some will start working on it.

■ During next lesson, students get working straight away; at the end of the lesson they set themselves targets for homework and the following lesson.

■ The next lesson peer assessment takes place and they reflect on the previously set targets.

■ Students continue working on the article; they act on the peer feedback and aim to achieve their self-set targets before final submission.

▪ After teacher feedback, they reflect on the learning process and set themselves transferable, long-term targets.

Having a clear routine for lessons is helpful for students, but don't feel you have to always comply. Be flexible when you need to be. You and the students will appreciate it at times.

4 Plan for feedback

The one strategy I've developed which has probably had the biggest impact on my work-life balance has been the careful planning of feedback and the meticulous incorporation of peer and self-assessment. It takes times to develop these skills with students, to help them to understand the advantages and to ensure they carry it out effectively so they and their peers benefit. However, it can pay off dividends in supporting both progress and your work-life balance.

In my initial days of teaching, every now and then I'd plan self or peer assessment into individual lessons, usually associated with answers that could easily undergo a bit of tick and flick or for extended answers. It'd be a simple bit of identifying what the student had done well and what they could do to improve. Rarely did students even read the feedback, let alone act on it.

I realise now that it was also rare that I considered how I'd mark or provide feedback over a prolonged period or how it would feed into other lessons. Although I used a variety of marking techniques in my first two years of teaching; I'd decide upon them as I sat down to or even whilst I marked a set of books.

In 2015, I finally started on the road to moving from marking to feedback. I found myself marking every night. On the weekends, to get through every class I taught once a fortnight. It was ridiculous and just couldn't be sustained. That's when I started to rebel, to find ways to reduce my marking workload and to think about how feedback could be used effectively.

For the first time since I started teaching, I started to carefully contemplate how feedback could be used effectively and how it could be used to reduce how much time I spent marking books outside of directed time. I considered how it would feed into what students do in the classroom and the work they produce, how it would feed into providing them with timely feedback and how it would then lead to progress.

This led to developing a feedback cycle that is often referred to as feed up-feedback-feedforward.

At first though, this meant I was triple marking work. I'd mark the work and provide feedback. Students would act on the feedback. I'd then mark the improvements again, if necessary leaving a question or target for students to respond to. They'd respond, and I'd assess their response for a third time. This was partly my fault for not considering how to embed this effectively but also a result of the school marking policy based on David Didau's work on Triple Impact

Marking. This approach was misguided and again unsustainable, not how David Didau had intended triple marking (Didau, 2014). Now I put more of the onus on the students, and it works.

Implementing a feedback cycle

A feedback cycle is a useful tool to develop student engagement with verbal and written feedback.

What is feedback-feedforward?

The role of feedback-feedforward cycles is to help the close the gap in learning and progress, to support students in reaching the end goal effectively over time.

Feedback provides students with information on where they are in relation to learning goals. It can be skills based or content based and should enable students to reflect and evaluate their progress, understanding and application of learning. On the other hand, feedforward then promotes action through constructive guidance on how to improve, and when provided with the opportunity to do so, the feedback becomes useful.

Feedforward should also relate to teacher instruction. We have to consider how what we learnt in the feedback process will influence our short, medium and long-term planning. The feedback-feedforward cycle should influence our future lessons. This does however mean we need to be flexible in our planning, to be willing to reteach and act on misconceptions.

Implementing feedback-feedforward

Implementing a feedback-feedforward approach to marking and assessment isn't easy. It takes carefully planning and organisation but is achievable with the right outlook and collaboration.

In the summer term sit down and look at the schemes of work you will be teaching in the coming year. Carefully plan out assessments to ensure they are spaced and identify pieces of work that can be self- or peer-assessed.

In my department is looks something like this:

As a team, we decided on the knowledge and skills we wanted students to develop over the course of school year. Next, we decided on the work we would then assess and distributed them carefully. We followed this by deciding which tasks would involve students responding to written feedback given to them through the feedback-feedforward cycles. Finally, we looked at who would carry out the assessment and provide feedback to the student. We wanted a blend of teacher and peer assessment over the course of the year.

Legend:

I&S assessment	Teacher-assessed	Peer- or teacher-assessed	Peer-assessed	FF Feedforward

Sept — Oct — Nov — Dec — Jan — March

Topic 1 – China – sustainable development

Describing and explaining population distribution	Knowledge test	One Child Policy info-graphic	Energy – sustainable development	Summative task National Geographic article project	Book Check
6 marks	Marks	B	C	A	RAG
FF	A	C	D / FF	D	

Topic 2 – Brazil – physical systems

Describing patterns	Describing and explaining cycles (either water, nutrient or carbon)	Biome presentation peer assessed	Biome presentation	Biomes homework task	Book check
4 marks	6 marks	B	B	A	RAG
FF	FF	C	C	FF	

April — May — June

Topic 3 – The Middle East – power and conflict

Describing and explaining patterns	Why is the Dead Sea shrinking?	Why is the Dead Sea shrinking? Feedforward	Critical thinking letter to the Government	Conflict homework project Peer Assessed	Book check
6 marks	A	A	C	B	RAG
FF	D	D / FF	D	C	

Figure 6.1 Example of assessed work across the school year for a single year group

In between teacher-assessed work, students would receive regular feedback from both their peers and the teacher. Most often teacher feedback was to be achieved through verbal feedback and whole-class feedback as well as feeding-up through modelling expected outcomes.

We've carried this out fully over one full year to date and it has proven successful at reducing crunch points of several assessments occurring in conjunction with one another. Whilst it is not perfect and we're sure several amendments will be made before it is, it has helped our work-life balance by reducing the overall amount of marking and assessment, giving students responsibility and emphasising verbal feedback in lessons.

If as a department or teacher, you don't have the autonomy to organise and disperse assessments, you can still consider the provision of feedback: how it'll be carried out, when it will take place and by whom. You'll also need to consider how it will influence future planning and the immediate and long-term opportunities for students to feedforward. If you train your students in the art of feedback, you can incorporate them into the process which inevitably supports their journey to becoming independent learners.

The key thing is to ensure students receive the opportunity to act on feedback and can feedforward in a timely manner. Here's how I implement the feedback-feedforward cycle and find it works with good effect:

- If formative and peer-assessed – same lesson or set as homework

- If formative and teacher-assessed – within a fortnight

- If summative and peer-assessed – same lesson or following lesson

- If summative and teacher-assessed – within a fortnight and set as a long-term target to apply at a later date

It is helpful for students to keep track of their long-term targets in a designated location in their book or folder. This makes for easy reference and tracking. I like to include a date set and dates achieved column that students are responsible for completing in the time provided in lessons.

5 Scaffold and model

As teachers, it is our responsibility to ensure that we support learners to overcome the barriers to their learning, whether they happen to be academic or pastoral. One way to do that is through differentiation. But too often differentiation focuses on providing a plethora of different support, worksheets or tasks for individual students each lesson. Thus, the associated workload becomes unrealistic and unsustainable.

So, when it comes to differentiation within lesson planning, try to focus on the use of modelling the task in advance of students partaking in it independently and scaffolding students to success.

From my experience to date, it has become far more sustainable and fruitful to differentiate by teaching to the top and scaffolding students to achieve the outcomes rather than providing individualised instruction to meet students' individual needs and learning methods.

Modelling helps to set out expectations, provides students with an objective and demonstrates to students the process. It can be carried out with the whole class or with individuals and small groups. As students become more proficient in the concept or skill, modelling can be scaled down and emphasis placed on scaffolding instead.

Scaffolding then involves the delivery of supportive, structured interactions or resources with the aim of helping students to achieve a specific goal. It involves the provision of temporary support strategies, that move students towards a level of competency and independence in the skill, concept or learning process. It is therefore possible for teachers to create a bank of general templates that can be amended to suit the content or level of competency of the student.

Whilst it is still important to implement strategies that support students general and specific learning needs, consider how applying them to everyone can benefit the few.

The chapter that follows explores differentiation and scaffolding in more detail.

Other time-saving ideas

Create a bank of activity templates

When you create a new resource, save an additional copy and remove all the subject-specific content. You then have a template for future use.

Use slide master to create template PowerPoints

If you use PowerPoint regularly, set yourself up with a customised slide master. This simply gives you a template for creating PowerPoints, meaning you can set slides to contain the same fonts, images, format, colours and so on. You can make changes to the Slide Master and they will be applied to all slides in your presentation. If you've not come across a Slide Master before, search for 'Slide Master Tutorial' and you will find plenty of helpful resources and how-tos to guide you in setting one up.

Organise your digital files

Create a folder for each topic, and for each lesson name all of the documents associated with it by its location in the topic sequence along with a brief description of it. See Figure 6.2 for an example.

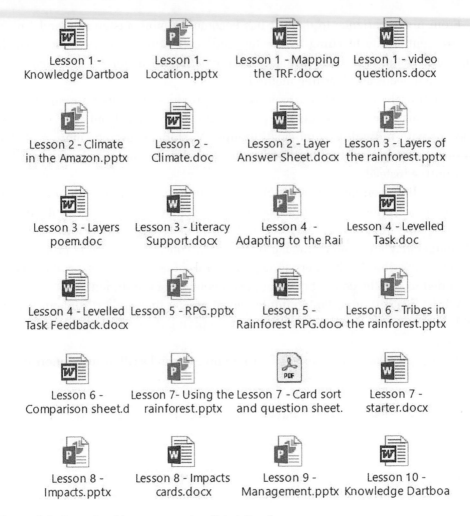

Figure 6.2 Example of how to organise digital files for easy access

This makes it much easier and less time consuming when locating files, particularly when you plan on using them again the following year.

It also helps if you are sharing resources with others, particularly non-specialists.

Refine, revise and reuse

Seriously, reuse resources as much as possible. If after using them you see areas for improvement, refine or revise the resource or activity before the next use; you don't need to start from scratch. Store resources in an organised way so that you can keep using them for years to come. It may sound like common sense, but the number of teachers I've witnessed throw resources away after one use is an environmental issue of its own.

Give students jobs

Give students the responsibility of a job or role in the classroom; anything from resource handler to card sort cutter, particularly if you have students using your room during breaktime or lunch. For example, I regularly give my form group the responsibility of setting up resources for the next lesson. Sometimes this involves collecting and sorting printing, cutting up resources, dividing up materials to tables and so on. A little reward in the way of house points and they are happy, whilst I've made time to get to the staff room for a cuppa. Win-win situation really.

Snippets of insight

I asked my EduTwitter colleagues the question, "When it comes to lesson planning, what advice would you give others to help reduce the time spent planning?" Here are there tips, advice and words of wisdom.

"First, that 'good enough' is exactly what it says: 'good enough'. We don't need to spend endless time hunting for a 'better' graphic for a resource etc. No one can be consistently outstanding: accept this. Keep it simple – unless your school requires a specific template to be used (and Ofsted doesn't) don't over-complicate". *Gill Rowland, Senior Lecturer at Canterbury Christ Church University. Tweets as @gillrowland1*

"Planning is very personal; it's important to try different strategies and work out what is best for you. The way you plan will change too as you gain experience and grow in confidence. I always start with the outcome in mind and build activities around it. How detailed the plan is would depend on my confidence, knowledge of the topic, time available and so other such factors". *Maria O'Neill, Pastoral leader for ESafety & PSHE; Founder @UKPastoralChat. Tweets as @DaringOptimist*

"Keep lessons lean – there's no need for lots of whizzy activities and resources. Focus on reviewing prior learning to aid retrieval, explaining and modelling well, giving time for deliberate practice and then assessing what students do or don't understand which will help to inform future lessons". *Rebecca Foster, Head of English. Tweets as @TLPMsF*

"Use good commercial schemes as a basis and annotate them. Don't waste time cutting and pasting or copying them into a school format, and if you have to, don't write thousands of words. It is for you. Your time is best spent on your resources and your presentation". *Andrew Cowley, Deputy Headteacher and author of 'The Wellbeing Toolkit' (May 2019). Tweets as @andrew_cowley23*

"Magpie ideas! Read around for great ideas, don't think everything needs to be invented by everyone independently. Remember too that great teachers guide students to do their own learning, so plan to get students active as soon as you can; they should be doing the bulk of the work. Build up a bank of techniques (which you constantly add to) allied with knowing your students always pay dividends, especially when you reflect honestly and act to improve". *Ed Brodhurst, Assistant Headteacher. Tweets as @brodhurst*

"Where possible, make answer sheets to worksheets and always file them for next year. Work collaboratively with other department members on new schemes of work and keep them in a file on the school system that all can access. Learn when to say 'good enough is good enough' and to close the laptop lid!" *Sarah Larsen, Teacher of Geography. Tweets as @sarahlarsen74*

"Don't reinvent the wheel. Look for well-designed schemes of work made by reliable organisations and teachers. For example, as a primary teacher, I often go to Nrich and NCETM for maths ideas, lessons and resources. I rarely create anything of my own from scratch now. Speak to colleagues and let them know what you need help planning with and learn from their experience and expertise. Buy them a pint or a glass of wine and you'll never need to spend ages planning again!" *Adrian Bethune, Teacher and author of 'Wellbeing in the Primary Classroom: A Practical Guide to Teaching Happiness'. Tweets as @AdrianBethune*

Takeaways

- What you write on paper doesn't determine and control what you do in the classroom. Respond there and then. Reflect after the lesson. Amend if you need to.

- Learning is a process. It requires flexibility. Don't be afraid to change your planned lesson, to take diversions or to make a stop and reteach.

- Plan backwards. Consider the big picture and the long-term process of learning rather than lesson by lesson.

- Create a learning routine, not necessarily a lesson routine.

- It's okay to use lessons and resources from others. Avoid reinventing the wheel; adapt them to suit your students.

- "Good enough is good enough", your resources don't need to look professionally made. Spend more time on the important things (both work and life related).

- Lessons don't need to be fun and exciting; a flamboyant lesson now and then will suffice. Learning should be enjoyed, not the activity.

- Build a learning toolkit. Research learning strategies, try a variety, create templates for those that work.

- Share and collaborate with others, whether it be internally or with teachers elsewhere. Work together to reduce the workload

References

Didau, D. (2014) *Why 'triple marking' is wrong (and not my fault)* [Online] Available at https://learningspy.co.uk/leadership/triple-marking-wrong-not-fault-2/ [Accessed 17th August 2018]

Griffith, A., & Burns, M. (2014) *Outstanding Teaching, Teaching Backwards.* Crown House Publishing, Carmarthen, UK.

Morrison McGill, R. (2018) *Mark. Plan. Teach. Save Time. Reduce Workload. Impact Learning* 1st ed. Bloomsbury Education, London, UK.

Smith, J. (2017) *The Lazy Teacher's Handbook: New Edition: How Your Students Learn More When You Teach Less.* Crown House Publishing, Carmarthen, UK.

UKEd Chat (2017) *Finished? Try one of these . . .* by @misstait_85 – @UKEdResources [Online] Available at https://ukedchat.com/2017/01/05/finished-try-one-of-these-by-misstait_85-ukedresources/ [Accessed 25th October 2018]

7 Differentiation and scaffolding

Each of our students will be different, not just in the way they look and their personalities or interests but in the way in which they learn and progress. Within any class there will be students at different stages of development: physically, mentally and academically. Their social and cultural experiences will differ, influencing their decisions and actions. Some will have barriers to learning or needs to address to ensure they access the learning, whilst others will whizz ahead with little support or guidance requiring challenge and extension.

As teachers we must therefore understand, pre-empt and deliver strategies to support and challenge all students in the learning process. We must meet students' needs over time to enable all students to enjoy success and to feel challenged, for us that means knowing and understanding how we can accommodate for each student.

During my first few years of teaching, I'd differentiate to an unsustainable level.

Teacher standard 5 is *"Adapt teaching to respond to the strengths and needs of all pupils"* and states that the teacher should *"know when and how to differentiate appropriately, using approaches which enable pupils to be taught effectively" Department for Education, 2011*

For a long while, my understanding of teaching standard 5 was that I needed to differentiate for student's individual needs, every lesson, whether these be their learning support needs such as those associated with an additional educational need or progress needs such as different target grades and levels.

On reflection, it was the fact that students (and I) had targets to achieve, which led to the exacerbated workload. For example, in a GCSE class, target grades meant I could have had students targeted E or D working alongside students targeted A or A*. I'd therefore be catering not only for individual learning support needs, but their individual progress needs as well. It felt like I'd be planning several lessons within a lesson through the provision of different levels of work and expected outcomes, different approaches to reach each outcome and different resources to support students. The case was similar in Key Stage 3 classes. However, all of this work did once get me the accolade of 'the Queen of Differentiation' by one of my former Headteachers.

Eventually, I came to understand the impossibility of this and inevitably it contributed to my burnout. Over time I've discovered that the best way to support students is to not only differentiate but to scaffold and model learning. The similarities between differentiation and scaffolding mean that often it is difficult to distinguish between the two as frequently they are found to be combined to support students and move them forward. Yet they are not synonymous.

What's the difference?

Differentiation refers to the concept of making provisions to alleviate barriers to learning because of each student's individual needs. Generally, it refers to the adaptations made to the teaching techniques and associated resources to cater for the range of different abilities, learning needs and interests of a class, all of which varies from student to student. Usually this means a greater degree of individualised materials for students.

Scaffolding, on the other hand, is the idea that structures are given to students to support and clarify the process to meet objectives. Scaffolding aims to makes students proficient at and independent in the learning process over time.

This therefore means that generally differentiation may result in each student accessing the end goal in a different way meaning a greater workload for teachers; whereas with scaffolding all students reach the goal in the same way but the support provided varies.

It's a blend of the two that leads to success.

Differentiation

"Differentiation is the process whereby teachers meet the need for progress through the curriculum by selecting appropriate teaching methods to match the individual student's learning strategies, within a group situation". Visser, 1993

My understanding of differentiation developed with research, action and curiosity. It was only after five years or so of teaching that I began to recognise how misconstrued my understanding of differentiation was in the first few years.

When I was training to teach, I learnt that differentiation was "the process by which differences between students are accommodated so that all students in a group have the best possible chance of learning" as described by the Training and Development Agency for Schools and that differentiation could be by task, support and outcome.

■ Differentiation by task involved setting different tasks for students of different abilities.

- Differentiation by support meant giving more help to certain students.

- Differentiation by outcome meant setting everyone the same task and allowing student response at different levels.

Differentiation is far more than this. It's a teacher's response to learner's needs and therefore can be planned or unplanned, long-term or short-term, explicit or subtle.

When it comes to differentiation, I'd go as far as to say it's misunderstood by a lot of practitioners, both new and experienced. I don't feel ITT gives sufficient time to developing our understanding of it, the variety of approaches and their implementation. It all comes with trial and error, experience and time, research and practice. In your formative years, seek out support in developing your understanding of what differentiation is and how you can implement it.

Once you discover and understand all the ways in which you might differentiate, you recognise that it is far more than just different tasks, worksheet or level of challenge, and as you become more effective at it, it eventually it becomes a lot less time consuming.

Common myths

The following myths are based on my experiences as well as the experiences of teachers both new and experienced that I have worked with.

"We must differentiate for every student, every lesson"

This is the most common myth, that I hear far too often. I'm going to say it loud and proud, THIS IS IMPOSSIBLE! Don't even try to differentiate for every strength, need or experience of every student, every lesson. It won't make you an outstanding teacher, it'll just make you an exhausted one.

You simply cannot differentiate for every student and every strength or need all of the time. Providing essential materials for specific needs such as overlays, printouts and the like, is very different to individualised differentiation. Instead being able to adapt and respond in the moment is just as important as planning appropriate approaches for key individuals in advance.

I've found that if you get to know your students well enough you begin to pre-empt the challenges that may arise, and you plan accordingly. If you know the subject content sufficiently, you start to identify where misconceptions generally occur, and when you understand which concepts and skills present the most difficulties then you come up with strategies to support students.

What's more important is then having a knowledge of different strategies to support and challenge and being able to deploy them as and when is necessary. This all comes with time and experience.

There are also times when you plan and prepare support materials and students won't require what you anticipated they would need. In other words, it is better to pre-empt and react than it is to plan and insist.

"Data tells us everything"

I hate data. There I said it. I look at it and I think "what does this really mean?" I can't be the only one. I use data, but I don't find it overly useful because data or a label can't possibly tell us everything we need to know about a student, their strengths, weaknesses, needs, interests, socio-economic background, cultural experiences and so on.

The only way you can do that is to talk to your students, assess their understanding and respond and adapt to their needs in the lesson. Use what you learn to plan accordingly.

As much as you can use data to plan for students with identified needs or of different levels of attainment, it doesn't necessarily correlate to what they need in that time and place. Each student is individual; what works for one may not work for another even when the data tells us they are they are the 'same'.

Be prepared to get to know your students, and keep brief notes on the effectiveness of strategies you use with them to get to know what strategies to deploy in future.

"Differentiation by outcome is not acceptable"

I can't remember if it was my first school or whether I'd learnt it on my PGCE course but in my formative years of teaching, I went by the rule 'differentiation by outcome is not acceptable'. Therefore, my original understanding of differentiation was that it meant providing different work for students based on their needs and abilities; they couldn't just be doing the same work but reach a different outcome with it. For instance, I couldn't give all students the same question, but some would answer it better than others.

Now I guess that meant providing students with different support materials to reach the same outcome as those that could do so independently. Yet in my first school, I also had to painstakingly produce lessons that had three levelled learning objectives, one that **all** students would achieve, one that **most** students would achieve and one that **some** students would achieve.

This meant that at times, I'd essentially be teaching multiple lessons in the same lesson to cater for the three learning objectives.

However, I've come to realise that's not how differentiation works. There's far more to it than that for instance, in geography and history at GCSE all students undertake the same questions; there is no differentiation between those doing higher tier and foundation. In statutory tests at primary level, they all sit the same questions too. Therefore, there is differentiation by outcome and that is perfectly acceptable in the classroom as well.

"Differentiation can be demonstrated in a lesson observation"

Differentiation will look different in every classroom, in every lesson. Adapting teaching in response to student's strengths and needs is a prolonged process and not always an easily recognisable one. The technique one might use with one student on one aspect of a topic, may not translate to another aspect of the topic or to another child.

It's not as simple as providing individual worksheets or setting up groups of different ability students as often this just isn't necessary. Technically, if differentiation is a teacher's response and accommodation to enable students to learn, then you can only plan differentiation to a degree. For students with an identified and specific need our pre-emptive planning and our response when needs arise are most important.

During a lesson observation, you may not even recognise that differentiation has occurred either from the position of the teacher or the observer. In fact, good differentiation is often discrete and embedded, making it difficult to pin-point and identify. We therefore need to change how we address differentiation, rather than looking for differentiation or asking what did you do to differentiate? We need to be asking what strengths appeared in students? How did you address this to challenge them further? What needs arose in students? How did you address this to support them?

If after an observation your asked to demonstrate differentiation, consider all the ways that differentiation can take place. For instance differentiation can be found in any of the following:

- The task

- The provision of resources

- Seating plan

- Groups

- Verbal Feedback

- Written Feedback

- Instruction

- Subject Content

- The process

- The outcome

- Level of challenge

- Questioning

- Assessment

- Dialogue with students

- Environment

- Rules and Routines

- Student choice

- Interests

- Student responsibilities

- Pastoral care

Essentially providing it involves the teacher acting and responding to their student's strengths and needs to enable all students to be taught effectively, then differentiation is taking place. It may not be evident to the observer at the time, so it's important to discuss the actions taken after the lesson has occurred but before any judgements are made.

"Differentiation is for individual students"

Differentiation doesn't need to be implemented on an individual basis; differentiated teaching can be applied to meet the needs of small groups as well. You may even differentiate within the whole-class situation.

Often once I've set up the task, I give students a moment to read the instructions and to start thinking about the task at hand. After a few minutes have passed, I will take a wander around the classroom and look for those that may be challenged by the task. I usually know who these will before I even look, but I give them time to try to figure it out before intervention. From there I will have strategies ready to go for the skills or concepts I know some students will find challenging and employ them in addition to the strategies I have in place for meeting-specific learning support needs.

Once you get to know your students, it becomes much easier to identify where support may be required, and the type of support students will require to meet the learning objectives. But to start with it helps if you implement a system that allows students to identify themselves to you. There have been numerous ways I have done this over the years from having a 'help me' table that students move to, the use of red cards on desks to indicate they need help or the old put your hand up and wait routine. You start to identify small groups of students that have similar needs and can start to bring them together as other students engage in the task. You can then work with a small group to deploy differentiated strategies to reduce the repetition of instruction or support whilst the others progress independently.

You can also use strategies aimed at particular students, that would also benefit others. For instance, one strategy I consistently use is the colours used for PowerPoint slides. After working on SpLD training with the SENCO at my first school, I discovered the benefits of pastel colours and off-white backgrounds for dyslexic and visually challenged learners. Now all of my PowerPoints follow the same colour rules, light grey background, pastel blue textboxes for information, pastel yellow for tasks and pastel orange for keywords. All fonts are dyslexic friendly and suitably sized. Not only does the same format help to organise the content and direct learners' attention to certain parts, it also reduces glare on the board and allows all students to access the presentation material.

"Differentiation is the responsibility of the classroom teacher"

I'm arguing this one because I don't just feel it is the sole responsibility of the classroom teacher. We must have an awareness of strengths and needs and be able to deploy teaching approaches that engage and support students to overcome the factors that inhibit one's ability to learn, but we also need the support of others in doing so.

- SENCOs must share information and suggest strategies to guide our practice, it's essential that SENCOs and those involved in the SEN team disseminate regular SEN updates to staff as new information comes to light about students and their needs.

- Pastoral support teams need to share and up-date staff on pastoral needs that will hinder a student's ability to learn.

- Teachers should collaborate, reflect on and share strategies that work for individuals, helping to give consistency to the support provided.

It is then our responsibility to use that knowledge in the best way possible.

"The real world won't be differentiated"

On the flip side, I have come across teachers that refuse to differentiate for individual student needs; arguing that when they are in the workplace their needs won't be catered for and thus they need to get use to that now. My argument here is that, as adults we are responsible and educated enough to make our own decisions and develop strategies to help us to get by. Also, when you consider the Equality Act, employers actually have a duty to make reasonable adjustments for those with a registered disability to which many additional learning needs would apply.

I won't get into the legal obligations for schools and teachers associated with the SEND code of practice, the Special Educational Needs and Disability Act 2001 or other legislation that provide plenty more reasons for why we should be differentiating in our classroom because its long and tedious. But what we need to consider is the fact that children and young people are learning, developing and becoming self-aware. They need suggestions and strategies to be provided to find what works for them, enabling them to apply such strategies later life. That doesn't mean we insist they use what we issue, but we give them the opportunity to try it, test it and assess its impact before determining whether to use it again in the future or bin it.

When support is provided to students we should discuss the influence with them to uncover its effectiveness and to identify potential amendments. This is where scaffolding comes in, the support is provided in a way that eventually students become independent in the learning process with an understanding of their own strengths and needs and how to apply strategies that support them to achieve.

Reducing the workload

The following are a series of every day differentiation strategies that can be applied to support all learners.

If you have students with a general or specific learning need that requires action to remove the barriers to enable successful learning, consider how you can put a strategy in place that will benefit them as well as all other learners in your classroom. It is highly unlikely that a strategy you use for students with SEN will be a barrier to other learners.

The following are strategies I make use of that have been successful for students I've taught over the years; they are mostly focused on general or specific learning difficulties rather than on social, emotional and behavioural difficulties as these tend to be more specific to the student and context.

Please remember I'm no expert in special education needs or differentiation for that matter; these are things I have discovered work through research and implementation. Your context, key stage and style will determine the effectiveness of such strategies, but maybe give some of them a go.

I Pastel colours

I've been using pastel colours for PowerPoints and other digital documents that are to be projected onto the whiteboard for a long time now. I read somewhere during my NQT year that pastel colours are preferable for students with dyslexia but are also beneficial for all students as white backgrounds can cause eye strain. To support this, I use a pastel yellow textbox for task instructions, blue for information and green for assessment for learning. In addition, the background is a light grey to reduce glare and sensitivity to bright lights. I sometimes adapt the colours if I have students with Irlen Syndrome to suit their preferential colours.

You can do the same for printed resources by using cream or pastel-coloured paper rather than white.

Further reading

Role and value of colour www.bdadyslexia.org.uk/dyslexic/eyes-and-dyslexia
    Supporting Irlen Syndrome https://irlen.com/what-you-can-do/

2 Simple design

Ever watched a presentation by a student with lots of whizzing text, different fonts and more colours than the rainbow? How did it make you feel? Was it easy to read? Probably not.

As tempting as it might be to include lots of different fonts, colours and animations, they can be a barrier to learning. Keep things simple. Simple backgrounds, limited colour, easy-to-read fonts.

In particular, consider the typefaces you use. To support all learners but particularly those with an SpLD need such as dyslexia use clear fonts such as Arial, Comic Sans, Century Gothic, Verdana, Trebuchet or Calibri. If you can, download one of the dyslexic friendly fonts such as Lexia Readable, Open-Dyslexic, Dyslexie. These fonts have good ascenders and descenders and clearly distinguish between b and d as well as p and q, making them easily accessible.

In addition, I would suggest the following:

- Avoid adding text effects such as reflections and shadows where possible.

- Try to avoid backgrounds with patterns or pictures that draw attention from the text.

- Do use dark-coloured text on a light background, but preferably not white

- There are some colours to avoid such as green, red and pink as these can be challenging for students with colour blindness

Further reading

BDA guidance www.bdadyslexia.org.uk/employer/dyslexia-style-guide-2018-creating-dyslexia-friendly content

3 Differentiate your seating plan

Once you get to know your students, it's worth investing time in carefully arranging your seating plan. Consider the strengths and needs of students, both academic and pastoral. Are there students that are more responsible? Are there students that require more attention? Are there students that are capable but lack confidence? Are there students with a calming effect on others? Interrogate your seating plan, look for ways students could support and develop each other to overcome any barriers to learning. Seat students in the location that works best for the learning and make the seating plan work for you.

In my second year of teaching, I was inspired by an observation I undertook in a mixed ability maths lesson, in a school with a relatively poor socio-economic background. After a set of exams, the teacher identified each students' strengths and weaknesses in the Maths GCSE course. He then changed the seating plan and grouped the students accordingly, with the aim that they could support each other as they continued through the course. With the student's permission, he also identified the strengths of each student to the class, enabling them to seek help from each other as and when it was needed. The students had grown accustomed to helping each other. They'd learnt to explain effectively and even found alternative ways to achieve the answer alternative to those taught by the teacher.

Now I know not every classroom will be like this, but use your students to help one another, to develop their independence and confidence in learning.

4 Note-taking strategies

Often students with general or specific learning difficulties can struggle when it comes to note taking; the challenge of listening and writing at the same time can be troublesome. It has also been noted that students with ADHD can experience similar issues.

It's important to remember that note taking won't be troublesome for all students. You'll need to be selective or give students the choice of support however, avoid expecting all students to take down important notes as you speak, as they watch a video or similar.

Firstly, it's important to teach students how to take notes before setting them off and to scaffold them to independence. But even after teaching students the how, it can still be troublesome for many, particularly those with general or specific learning difficulties.

Some strategies to try to develop note-taking skills

- Stop, write and continue

  - Pause for a moment to give students time to think and write down relevant notes before continuing to talk or playing the video.

- Pens down

  - Instead of writing notes as information is given, students merely listen. They then have time at the end to discuss and write down the relevant information.

- Sticky notes

  - Instead of trying to take down lots of information, students merely write words, phrases and numbers. Students are given time to discuss the information and the relevance of what is on their sticky note before committing it to notes in their books or folders.

- Outline it

  - Students with SpLD and other SEN can find organising and sequencing information challenging, make it clear for them and rest of the class by providing note-taking sheets that outline the relevant content students should be paying attention too.

- Laminated template

  - In my classroom, I keep a bank of laminated, generalised note-taking templates that students can write on with a whiteboard pen. The ability to wipe it away helps students to overcome the fear of committing pen to paper in case of getting it wrong. The sheets also have a clear structure for notes with sections that do not require students to write down large amounts.

- Roles

  - Give students roles when it comes to note taking, such as a specific aspect of the content to note down, students can then share their findings with one another to complete the full picture. Alternatively, if students work in groups, note taking can be the responsibility of one or two students whilst the others contribute additional findings. Those not responsible for notes can be given a responsibility that caters to their strengths. I tend to use this strategy sparingly though as it can produce disproportionate responsibility.

- Printouts

  - Provide students with printouts of any presentations to annotate with additional key information.

5 Knowledge organisers

These provide students with an outline of the key content of the topic or subject area such as keywords, names, dates, processes, theory etc. Knowledge organisers can provide students with a reference point when taking notes and depending on the age and ability of the students can be used in a variety of ways. They are also effective for word retrieval, decoding difficulties and supporting learners with weak working memory. When creating knowledge organisers, teachers should consider the organisation of the information carefully ensuring clarity, to enable students to recognise links between the content and to support students to organise their thoughts and ideas.

Scaffolding

Nowadays, what I find most beneficial to students is scaffolding them to achieve their best, providing strategies that support them and that challenge them as they do so rather than lots of differentiated tasks and activities.

Jerome Bruner, a cognitive psychologist, described scaffolding as "the steps taken to reduce the degrees of freedom in carrying out some task so that the child can concentrate on the difficult skill she is in the process of acquiring" (Bruner, 1978).

Scaffolding involves guiding and modelling the process to students until they reach a point whereby the scaffold can be removed, and they can work independently with the knowledge that if they need it, resources are there to support them. This I believe is also the role of a Teaching Assistant, to help students until they are sufficiently independent to work without one. How long this takes will vary for each student in our care; some will never reach this point before the end of compulsory schooling. All we can do is our best to help them on the journey to becoming an independent learner.

Scaffolding strategies may include some of the following:

■ Keyword lists and vocabulary sheets

● These sheets outline the essential vocabulary students must be able to understand and apply to their work to demonstrate their full understanding of the learning taking place.

Humanities Key Terminology Lists

General geography	General history	Other terminology
Processes	Time Period	Scale
Human	Anno Domini (AD)	County
Physical	Millennium – 1000 years	Country
Social	Century – 100 years	Continent
Socially	Decade – 10 years	Local
Culture	Evidence	National
Economic	Primary	International
Economy	Secondary	Global
Wealth	Source	Continents
Income	Knights	Europe
Environmental	Mediaeval	Asia
Environment	Conqueror	Africa
Political	Defeated	North America
Politics	Invade	South America
Globalisation	Throne	Oceania/ Australasia
Nationality	Conflict	Antarctica
Sustainable	Infantry	Oceans
Sustainability	Defence	Pacific Ocean
Conservation	Warfare	Atlantic Ocean
Management	Cause	Indian Ocean
Development	Consequence	Arctic Ocean
Industry	Continuity	Southern Ocean
Industrial	Interpret	Seas and Channels

Figure 7.1 Example of keyword lists for Key Stage 3

General geography	General history	Other terminology
Services	Argue	Mediterranean Sea
Raw materials	Oral (spoken)	North Sea
Resources	Verbal (spoken)	English Channel
Renewable	Written	*Places of Interest*
Non-renewable	Image	North Pole, Arctic Circle
Fossil fuels	Artefact	South Pole, Antarctica
	Understand	Pompeii, Italy
		Hawaii, Pacific Ocean
		Amazon rainforest, Brazil
		Sahara Desert, Northern Africa
		Siberia, Russia

Figure 7.1 (Continued)

■ Knowledge organisers

- As mentioned previously these are sheets that outline the essential knowledge students must understand and apply in their learning. They can be completed in advance for the student as a differentiation tool or in order to scaffold, formatted and left blank for the student to fill in as and when they cover the content, providing them with a revision tool at the end.

■ Sentence structure mats

- These are great for developing literacy in lessons. They simply provide students with a variety of writing prompts for sentences with different purposes such as conjunctions to explain or evaluate.

■ Structure strips

- These are strips of paper that students glue into the margin. They provide the structure to format an answer. These can be differentiated easily by including more or less guidance. Structure strips can be created for a variety of skills you wish students to develop such as description, explanation and evaluation and can be generalised templates or content specific.

■ Graphic Organisers

- These are useful tools that help students to organise their thoughts and ideas, to plan an answer or to provide a visual display of information. They effectively encourage duel-coding, by allowing students to process information in multiple forms. There are a wide variety of templates freely available online so you don't even have to make them.

Population

Key Terms

Population – the inhabitants of a particular place
Development – the process of change and improvement
Economic – to do with money, jobs and finances
Social - to do with peoples everyday live, community and culture
Political – to do with government and how a place if run/governed
Environmental – to do with the natural world and the surroundings

MEDC – More economically developed country   **LEDC** – Less economically developed country
HIC- High income country   **LIC** – Low income country

Birth rate - The number of births per year per 1000 people
Death rate - The number of deaths per year per 1000 people
Life expectancy - The average age that people are expected to live until
Gross Domestic Product (GDP) - Total money produced per year by a country divided equally among the population
Fertility rate – The average number of children a women has in her life

Human – things or influences that are man-made

Employment – relates to jobs and work
Industry – economic activity concerned with the processing of raw materials and manufacture of goods in factories
Communications – ways of sending or received information, such as telephone lines or computers

Physical – naturally occurring things or influences

Relief – shape of the land (steep, gentle, flat, high).
Climate – the average weather conditions for a place.
Resources – the availability of supplies to meet human needs (e.g. coal, oil, gas, water, food).

Ageing Population – a population with a high proportion of people aged 65 and over.
Youthful Population - a population with a higher proportion of people under the age of 16.
Overpopulation – too many people in an area and there are not enough resources to support them.

Dense population – lots of people, usually crowded over 1km²

Sparse population – very few people, usually spread out over 1km²

Population Pyramid – a diagram to show the age and sex structure of a population.

Figure 7.2 Example of a knowledge organiser for Key Stage 3

Sentence Starters

To describe:
The diagram shows...
The map shows...
The picture shows...
The graph shows...
It shows...

To explain:
This happens because...
This demonstrates...
The processes causing this are...
Therefore...
This maybe because...

To give examples:
For example...
Such as...
For instance...
To illustrate...
...as an example...

To give opinions:
I feel...
I believe...
In my opinion...
It would seem that...
I suggest...

To summarise
In conclusion...
In summary...
In conclusion...
Overall...
Therefore...
Ultimately...

To add ideas:
Also...
As well as...
Furthermore...
More importantly...
Equally important...
In addition...

To connect ideas:
At first... then...
Secondly...
This is linked to...
As a result...
For that reason...
The effect is...

To compare and contrast:
Similarly...
In the same way...
However...
Then again...
In contrast...
This is in contrast to...

To show sequence/process: Firstly... Secondly... Thirdly...
To start with... Lastly... Finally... Eventually... Next... Meanwhile... Afterwards... Results in...

Connectives

and   but   if   yet   so   also   like

therefore   because   however   although   whereas   instead   otherwise

Figure 7.3 Example of a sentence starter mat for Key Stage 3

Weather in the UK is becoming more extreme – To what extent do you agree with this statement?	Weather in the UK is becoming more extreme – To what extent do you agree with this statement?
Introduction Define 'extreme weather'. Give examples. Outline your basic opinion.	**Introduction** Extreme weather is . . . Examples of extreme weather include . . . In my opinion I believe. . .
In support of Provide evidence to support that weather in the UK is becoming more extreme. Use your case studies.	**In support of** Weather in the UK is becoming more extreme because in . . . . This resulted in. . . . Another example includes. . . This caused . . .
Against Discuss why weather might not be becoming more extreme in the UK – consider the factors we discussed.	**Against** However, on the other hand, our weather may not be getting more extreme and instead . . . (consider measuring and recording, length of records etc.)
Conclusion Summarise your discussion. Make a judgement to the extent you agree/disagree with the statement. Justify the judgement.	**Conclusion** In summary . . . Overall, I agree/disagree with statement that the weather in the UK is becoming more extreme because . . .

Figure 7.4 Example of structure strips for Key Stage 4

Discussing differentiation

It's vital to talk to students about the support they receive to help them to understand how they learn best, to figure out the strategies that work effectively for them. There's no point in responding to student needs with strategies that have little to no impact.

Growing up I had speech and language difficulties. Instead of being asked about the strategies that teachers would implement, I was just expected to follow. I struggled particularly with spelling; in fact, I still do but did anyone ever ask me what helps me to learn to spell. No, never.

The only strategy I ever remember is read, cover and write. It wasn't until I was in year 10 that I figured out that the strategy that worked best for me was writing the word out how I thought it ought to be spelt, then searching for the word in

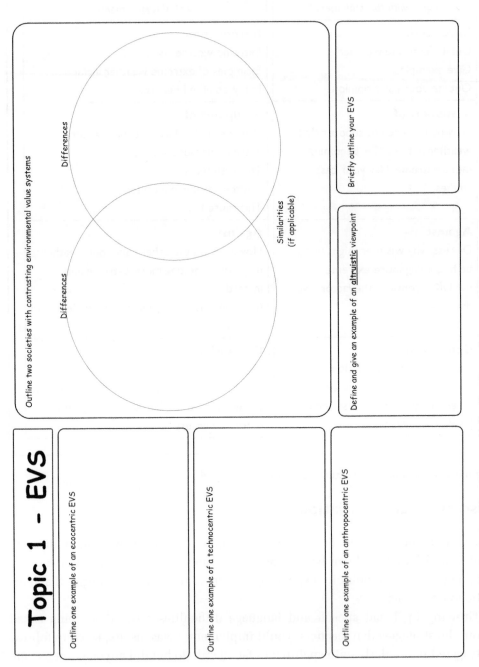

Figure 7.5 Example of graphic organisers for Key Stage 5

the dictionary. Although it would on occasions take me a while, the practice of searching for and reading the definitions helped me to remember the spelling and also developed my vocabulary in the process.

If my teachers had asked me if the read, cover and write routine worked I'd have said no, we could have tried something else. Do make sure you talk to your students about the support you put in place no matter how young or old they are because didn't someone once say, insanity is doing the same thing over and over again and expecting different results?

Snippets of insight

This time I asked my Twitter colleagues "What differentiation strategies do you find most useful and least time consuming?" The insights provided on differentiation have a lot of cross-over yet there are also some divergent views. You do not have to agree with any or all of them, but there are useful tips and hints to takeaway.

"Differentiation by outcome can be acceptable. If I am teaching persuasive devices, there can be a number of different ways to demonstrate understanding. Differentiation by input can be done by 'chunking' students together. You don't have to meet everyone's needs all the time – but over time". *Gill Rowland, Senior Lecturer at Canterbury Christ Church University. Tweets as @gillrowland1*

"Knowing your class or classes really well is the best differentiation tool. It means I will know which children might need a bit more support from me, it means I can pair children up that I think will support one another, it means I can predict (somewhat) what the misconceptions might be before they arise and teach to correct them. Sometimes I'll differentiate via the task, sometimes by the support I give but knowing your class is essential to knowing how to respond to their differing needs". *Adrian Bethune, Teacher and author of 'Wellbeing in the Primary Classroom: A Practical Guide to Teaching Happiness'. Tweets as @AdrianBethune*

"It is impossible to plan for each child. You can anticipate who will have a problem, but you can't anticipate every question and if you get diverted from your plan, that is good teaching. The most useful tool is getting all students to master the basics: knowledge organizers and recap testing of the basics helps with this. A good textbook also allows students to move on at their own pace". *Rufus Johnstone, Lead Coach. Tweets as @rufuswilliam*

"A useful strategy is setting those that confidently understand and are independent off on their own after minimum input, allowing you to focus on those that need the support first. Least useful strategy is the production of an individual plan for each student". *Andrew Cowley, Deputy Headteacher and author of 'The Wellbeing Toolkit' (May 2019). Tweets as @andrew_cowley23*

"Differentiation doesn't mean that any students should be doing something intrinsically different from everybody else in the room. Instead teach to the top and scaffold where appropriate; offer support where there's a need". *Rebecca Foster, Head of English. Tweets as @TLPMsF*

"Differentiation for me is as simple as 'challenge for all, support where needed'. I make sure every task in every lesson has a high level of challenge and I always circulate during tasks, offering support to the students who ask for help and to those who I know might need some scaffolding". *Jo Morgan, Maths Lead Practitioner, Harris Federation and UK Blog Award Winner 2017. Tweets as @mathsjem*

"It is not true that every task should be differentiated for all groups in all lessons – it simply isn't sustainable. Students will take different routes to the lesson objectives; don't get all students to work their way to the more challenging tasks. Higher order thinking tasks developed through Anderson's taxonomy is a good way to start doing this". *Ed Brodhurst, Assistant Headteacher. Tweets as @brodhurst*

"Teach up and scaffold down. Use targeted, differentiated questioning in class. Provide sentence starters for those that need them. Stretch and challenge activities (not just 'more of the same') for higher attaining students". *Sarah Larsen, Teacher of Geography. Tweets as @sarahlarsen74*

Takeaways

- It is impossible to plan for every student's need or strength, every lesson.

- Differentiation is more than just different tasks for different students; it's an ongoing process that involves a teacher's response to allow learning to take place for all.

- Differentiation is more sustainable when you teach to the top and differentiate down.

- Students will take different routes to the same outcome, scaffold to support and challenge.

- Discuss the strategies you use with your students to assess what works for them.

- Facilitate students to find what works for them.

References

Bruner, J. S. (1978) The Role of Dialogue in Language Acquisition. In: A. Sinclair, R. J. Jarvelle, & W. J. M. Levelt (Eds.), *The Child's Concept of Language*. New York: Springer-Verlag.

Department for Education (2011) *Teachers' standards* [Online] Available at www.gov.uk/government/publications/teachers-standards [Accessed 24th March 2018]

Visser, J. (1993) *Differentiation: Making It Work*. Tamworth: NASEN.

8 Behaviour and classroom management

Behaviour can be a source of stress and workload unto itself. It's often forgotten how hard it is to manage behaviour in the first few years of teaching by more experienced staff. Not only are you still getting to grips with pedagogy, subject content and teaching in general, but you also have to build up relationships, respect and a reputation. When you're trying to balance both aspects to ensure sufficient progress from your students, behaviour that is not conducive to learning can really start to stress you out especially if it is regular and persistent. Yet the positive is that rarely is it the direct result of student behaviour that causes teachers to walk away from the profession.

My NQT was full of difficult behaviour; I certainly experienced my fair share of disruption. The first thing that made it more bearable was knowing I wasn't the only one. Teaching assistants would comfort me at the end of lessons and reassure me that the behaviour wasn't towards me in particular, and that the students were like this for everyone or other members of staff. The second was that SLT were supportive and would take action when necessary. Whilst the support was reassuring, it didn't make it any less annoying or time consuming to deal with.

During the formative years, I found it most upsetting when I'd spent a significant amount time planning what I thought was an amazing lesson and then the behaviour would take a turn for the worse. Before I knew it, I'd be changing the lesson plan, often meaning that rather than teaching I was crowd controlling a classroom of teenagers. I hated every moment of it, the insisting on silent working conditions, showing my disappointment, calling for behaviour support, requesting students be removed from the classroom, anything I could do for the benefit of the other learners.

I'd be kept awake at night, worrying about the classes I had the next day because last lesson student a couldn't be trusted to sit next to student z without stealing their pen, whilst student b was throwing things across the room at student y all whilst I talked to student c at my desk because they were crying after student x had called them something derogatory. How was I to juggle so many situations at once whilst ensuring learning took place for those not involved? It felt like I spent most of the night thinking of every possible scenario and solution to manage the potential situations.

Then there would be the aftermath of behaviour in the classroom, I was regularly giving up breaks for detentions or chasing up students that failed to attend, calling home to parents to discuss the prolonged behavioural issues and the impact on progress or even having meetings with parents and students to discuss my concerns about their progress. And then in some cases I found that the parents weren't even supportive; it all ended in me feeling deflated and hopeless, and the cycle would begin again the next week.

The hours I spent dealing with behaviour in my first year are uncountable but throughout I tried my darn hardest to always be consistent and followed school procedures so much so that by the second year, my reputation had developed and fewer students pushed the boundaries. I'd also learnt a lot over that time and knew when to interject sooner. I became aware of the little indicators that would initiate low-level disruption. All of which came with time, patience and commitment.

And then I moved schools, and the whole process started again. Different students, different issues, different behaviour. I simply applied what I'd learnt the first time around and stuck with it.

If you find behaviour challenging at all, please do not worry or let it force you to leave. So long as you are proactive, consistent and committed to improving it, it does get better. As long as you are consistent, have clear expectations and follow the school procedures, your reputation develops, and you do see improvements year on year.

Top tip: try anything

The first few years of teaching are about mastering the art and developing your pedagogical approach. Try anything to manage behaviour but be consistent and fair.

In my first four years of teaching, behaviour was challenging at both the schools I worked at, yet the behavioural challenges were so different. This meant that the strategies I'd developed at the first school weren't always effective at the second. It's important to remember that It takes time to master behaviour, so if you don't crack it straight away don't punish yourself over it. Seek advice, watch good practice and be persistent.

My first piece of advice in relation to behaviour to ITT students and NQTs I've worked with is always don't worry about progress in the first term; use the first term to get to know your students and build the relationships that help to hinder behavioural issues. Set your routines and expectations and repeat them time and time again until your students know them. Be consistent in your approach and set sanctions if you need to.

Tips for managing behaviour

The following are ideas and strategies you may wish to try to help manage behaviour.

- Carefully consider your seating plan.

  - From day one with any class, put them in a seating plan. Not only does it help to learn names, it demonstrates that it is your classroom. Inform students that the seating plan is not permanent and will change. As to when it will change, don't divulge such information; that way if the current plan isn't working, students can't turn around with "but you said". Kids always surprise me with how astutely they actually listen.

- Welcome students.

  - Where possible strive to greet students at the door, develop general chit-chat with them, compliment and praise on their way in and just generally give a warm welcome to your classroom. Show them you want them to be there.

- Reward and praise selectively.

  - This one may be controversial, but praise and reward when it is worthy. Basically you need to ensure it maintains its value. Carefully consider the language you use, show students you appreciate their efforts, progress and choices. But do they need to receive a stamp for sitting down? Highlight students that are doing as expected and initially ignore those that are not.

- Have private rather than public conversations about behaviour.

  - Sometimes the teacher's reaction is all students want out of a situation – to see the teacher angry, frustrated and shouting at the class. Other times it's simply because they are struggling but don't want to ask for help. Have a quiet conversation with students when possible, avoid escalation and redirect students to the work. I strive to use the technique of explaining why I have had to speak to the student, what the outcome will be if they choose to continue, and then I ask them about the work. It is only when I discuss the work that I expect a response from the student. At this point I check their understanding and go through the instructions again, answering any questions they have. This hasn't always worked, but practice and experience has helped.

- Develop a classroom routine.

  - The consistency of a classroom routine helps to settle students. It means that I just need to remind them of the routine rather than discuss behaviour initially. For instance, when a rowdy group enter the lesson late, I simply remind them that we come in quietly, collect our books and get started with the task on the board. Usually this works, but not always.

■ Know your school, department or individual behaviour expectations, rules and sanction stages.

● It's vital you know the expectations, rules and sanctions clearly. It makes it much easier when dealing with behaviour. At my current school, I'll admit I didn't expect any behaviour situations when I started. Before starting, I therefore hadn't fully got to grips with the school behaviour policy and the sanction stages. I regretted this when a few students started to push the boundaries like most teenagers will at some point. I responded in my own way rather than following the school procedures. Erroneous. It meant I undermined myself by not knowing the whole-school consequential procedures and sanctions. Ensure you know them well before starting at a new school to ensure you are consistent with other staff.

■ Don't be afraid to seek support from other members of staff, this is not a weakness.

● Ask everyone and anyone for advice, ideas and help in the classroom if you're experiencing issues with behaviour. Do not fear it. You won't be the first and you certainly won't be the last to experience challenging behaviour.

■ Display and refer to expectations for behaviour, sanctions and school rules as and when required. Ensure they are clear and attainable.

■ Offer a student-led praise system, either across your school or within your classroom. Allow students to nominate one another for positive learning behaviours, creating a culture of high expectations as a result.

■ Hold high expectations.

● I was once told I was stressed because my expectations were too high. It made me furious because if I didn't believe they could participate in the work set, if I didn't believe they could behave, if I didn't believe they would succeed in the end, then why would they? Don't let anyone tell you your expectations of students are too high; instead support students to meet them. It might be difficult for a while, but they'll thank you later. It might be when they've left school, have their own kids and are employed but they will be appreciative of your time and effort in the end. As long as your expectations are attainable, believe your students can and will achieve them.

Reducing the workload

Reducing the workload surrounding behaviour is a challenge and is completely dependent on your context. I agree that detentions should be set through a centralised system so that teachers do not lose their breaks, but it still needs teachers to record and monitor and such systems require school leadership implementation.

But here are a few ways to reduce the personal workload:

- Set a time to record behaviour infringements each day so it doesn't eat into the time set for doing other things.

- Keep a bank of behaviour comments and copy and paste, edit with specifics if necessary

- If you have to deliver you own detentions, set them on a particular day of the week so you don't lose out on additional breaks.

- Print consequence slips that just require you to add a date, time, place and potentially reason. These can be given to students, parents and carers or glued into student planners.

Takeaways

- Emphasise the positive rather than negative behaviours.

- Know your own and school expectation, policies and procedures well and apply them consistently.

- Seek out advice when it needed.

- Never fear you are alone in experiencing negative behaviour.

- Encourage a centralised system to ensure staff receive the breaks they are entitled too.

9 Marking and feedback

I started to get into exploring marking and feedback back in 2015. Since then I've loved researching feedback and developing strategies that reduce the workload associated with marking but still provide high quality, effective feedback to students. Personally, I've found that an effective feedback cycle to be one of the most valuable strategies to improve progress and to close the gap within my classroom. Nevertheless it has taken time, enthusiasm and commitment to get there.

In my early-career days, I marked because I had to. There was an understanding within of its value to assess learning, to identify gaps and close them, but I never really understood how to do it effectively to get the most out of the process. Marking was a burden. Hours would be spent every day slaving over it, yet its impact was minimal.

It wasn't until the workload reached critical limits that I felt something had to change. I started researching and testing different strategies, not just in terms of marking but in terms of feedback as a whole. As I did so, I came to realise that not all feedback comes in the form of marking, something I never felt was covered during ITT training or the NQT year.

Over the first five years, I've been through a range of marking policies, most of which the emphasis has been on the teacher to give feedback via marking of books. Yet I found these have been the least effective, that could be down to experience or it could be the policy in place. Nowadays I have greater autonomy over how feedback is given in my classroom and throughout my department. This has meant feedback has become more effective. I spend less time marking and more time planning and greater emphasis is placed on the student rather than the teacher.

By emphasis on the student, I mean students take more ownership of their feedback. It's not something that is done to them and instead is something that they do. They participate in the process and understand the value of it.

The table below demonstrates some of the marking policies I experienced during my first five years of teaching. I've found the policy with the most autonomy to be the most effective to date.

Year of Experience	Marking Strategy	Prescribed by whole-school policy	Emphasis on . . .	Student response expected	Frequency
PGCE year	Two stars and a wish	Yes	Teacher	No	n/a
Year 1 (NQT)	WWW and EBI comments, RAG rating of progress towards the lesson objective	Yes	Teacher	Personal target setting only after assessments	Every four lessons
Year 2	WWW and EBI comments	Yes	Teacher	Personal target setting only after assessments	Every four lessons
Year 3 & 4	WWW and Next Steps comments, triple marking	Yes	Teacher/ Student through DIRT	Yes	Every four lessons
Year 5	Successes, next steps	No	Student	Yes	Select pieces of work

Figure 9.1 Marking policies experiencing during first five years of teaching

But why is feedback important?

The value and importance of high-quality feedback is evident in many studies as is the impact of different types of feedback including verbal and written. The Education Endowment Foundation (EEF) notably found that high-quality feedback can lead to an average of eight additional months progress over the course of a year, making it the tool with the greatest impact on progress in their Teaching and Learning Toolkit (Education Endowment Foundation, 2018)

John Hattie, a prominent academic in the field of feedback, has published multiple reports, journals and books on the importance of feedback; through which he has demonstrated and discussed that the most effective forms of feedback comes from those that provide cues to develop or reinforce current endeavours in knowledge, cogitative process or application of skills to learners, that are instructional and that relate to goals. Whilst the least effective are those that give little to no direction such as programmed instruction, praise and extrinsic rewards (Hattie & Timperley, 2007).

Additionally, feedback doesn't have to just be carried out by the teacher, high quality "feedback can take a range of different forms, including written feedback in the form of marking, oral feedback and peer feedback" (Elliott et al., 2016). Students need feedback to understand where they are, where they are going and how they can get to the desired outcomes; essentially feedback should be treated as a road map to learning to show students the way to success.

Feedback is often considered to be about closing the gap between where a student is and where they need to be in the learning process. However it is also about developing our students' ability to self-regulate, assess and reflect to become independent, self-directed lifelong learners.

In a feedback-friendly classroom, feedback also builds a platform for social and academic interactions. I love overhearing those moments when a student turns to another and explains to them what they have achieved and what they could do to improve the piece of work. Since the implementation of ACE feedback, I've heard more and more of these discussions and found that as the year progresses, students develop high-quality assessments of their work and that of their peers. Although peers can never take the place of the teacher, being able to give constructive feedback to one another enables them to access timely and meaningful feedback.

What is high-quality feedback?

High-quality, effective feedback is not just about marking books and assessing learning. Often feedback is merely seen as something imparted by the teacher, I think Deborah McCallum, author of *The Feedback Friendly Classroom* describes this perception well "the teacher directs, instructs, and imparts knowledge and feedback to the students; the student then follows this feedback to achieve the highest outcome" (McCallum, 2016). This was certainly the case for me in my formative years. I'd set a task; I'd mark the task. I'd say where the student did well and how they could improve. At a later stage they might have acted on the feedback. The problem here is that effective feedback is a series of strategies that are taught, modelled and implemented by both the teacher and students.

High-quality, effective feedback ought to be embedded into the fabric of the classroom, into the pedagogy of each lesson. Learning to do so, is practice changing. When feedback is embedded effectively it becomes far more than just marking.

- Feedback is an essential part of the teaching and learning process and thus ought to be a part of every lesson.

- Feedback is a two-way system and an ongoing process between students and their teacher.

- Feedback is integrated into assessment of and for learning over time.

- Feedback is part of the communication system, built upon exchange and interactions between all stakeholders in the classroom.

- Feedback is the foundation of planning, through feedback students are informed of their progress whilst the teacher provided with valuable information to influence their planning.

- Feedback is not solely a result of marking or written comments and can present itself in a variety of formats, written marking being just one element of it and the value of verbal feedback needs to be recognised.

How does this translate to the classroom?

Translating the above bullet points into my classroom practice, has been a learning curve and a long-term process. It doesn't just happen with immediate success. Instead it takes time, patience and some trial and error; but persistent implementation, reflection and adaptation pays off in the end. A feedback cycle in my classroom goes something like this:

Feed up

Before setting up a task, the purpose and objectives are made clear whether this be through examples, success criteria or demonstrating the process. Through modelling students develop an understanding of what they are aiming to achieve, and high expectations are initiated. In John Hattie's work this would be referred to as the 'feed-up' stage, the point at which students consider where are they going and what the goals of the task are.

Set off

Students are then set off. Some will immediately receive differentiated materials such as notes or instructions on coloured paper or keyword lists, but generally at this stage no one receives additional support specific to the task. Instead students are given the opportunity to contemplate the task and attempt to figure out how they will achieve the expected result independently or with their peers. At this point, I circulate the room and can usually determine by student behaviour those that are confident in the task and those that may require some support. At this point I will start to engage in conversation with students. Some students will be offered differentiated resources or support scaffolds to get them on their way, whilst others will independently go and collect materials.

Feedback

Through questioning and discussions with students, I am provided with feedback on how they are progressing. Using metacognitive questioning students are encouraged to monitor, evaluate and reflect on the learning process. In John

Hattie's work this would be referred to as the 'feedback' stage, the point at which students and the teacher see the "progress being made towards the goal" (Hattie & Timperley 2007).

The feedback I then through receive is used to continue or amend instruction; sometimes this might result in stopping the class and modelling again or asking students to give each other advice to overcome challenging areas. Following on, students will be expected to self-assess their work through proofreading and peer-assess using the ACE strategy.

Feedforward

After feedback from peer assessment, students make improvement or amendments to their work before submitting it as complete. I then assess the work and provide feedback. In John Hattie's work this would be referred to as the 'feed-forward' stage, the point at which there is consideration of the consequential actions that must follow for further progress to occur. Finally, students use the feedback to make improvements in a timely manner and to set targets for future application. At the same time, I use the feedback to modify my instruction and to influence future planning. Not only does the feedback feed into the work I do with current students, it feeds into the work carried out with future students. The great thing about feedback is it's a constant cycle; what you learn one year can be translated into the development of the following year.

For example, a few years ago, it came to light that a common misconception among students is that extreme weather and tectonic hazards such as earthquakes are related phenomena. It wasn't until I taught tectonics for the first time that I understood this misconception. The following year, instead of waiting for students to ask, I was able to address it in the initial lessons reducing the number of students that addressed it in the same task the following year.

Opportunity to think

As you assess work and gather feedback on learning consider the following:

- What aspects of the learning process were successful and should be continued?
- What aspects require change, either through a different approach or alteration of the current approach?
- Is there anything that requires re-teaching?
- Were there any common errors or misconceptions?
- How can errors and/or misconceptions be addressed now and in future?

The problem with marking and feedback

During workshops, I like to as participants, 'what's the problem with marking?' Every time, it's very similar responses that arise. These are the most common responses
Let us take a look at some of these issues.

Marking policies

All too often what I hear is that marking policies are unsustainable, excessive and lack autonomy. Usually they have been created by a senior leader with little to no input from teaching staff. On many an occasion, the research and evidence that might be used to underpin such policies has been misconstrued leading to unattainable marking requirements for staff. In particular, I've found that the emphasis on written comments in books has led to anguished, demotivated and discontent teachers.

If we take triple marking for instance, the concept being that the teacher marks students' work, they act upon it and the teacher marks the work again thus creating a dialogue with the student. When David Didau first wrote about and endorsed Triple Impact Marking, a system developed by Clevedon School, what he envisaged was "students self-assess their work, you mark their work, they respond to your marking" (Didau, 2014), thus, putting the onus on the student. Instead, in many cases what we have seen is meaningless dialogue that has led to valuable time being wasted in the classroom.

Other examples of misconstrued marking policies include:

- Marking every piece of work

- Extensive written comments

- Recording of verbal feedback

- Student/Teacher written dialogue

- Deep marking

Time constraints

The time it takes to mark a set of books for some subjects versus the impact it has on learning and progress is often discussed. Marking and the assessment of learning is an essential element of the feedback process however the time it takes, and the ineffective nature of many marking methods often deem it a waste of time, particularly as the time taken is not repaid in terms of the impact on student progress.

Additionally, the time taken to mark is far too excessive in comparison to the direct time available. For example, Key Stage 3, classroom teachers and middle

What's the issue with marking?

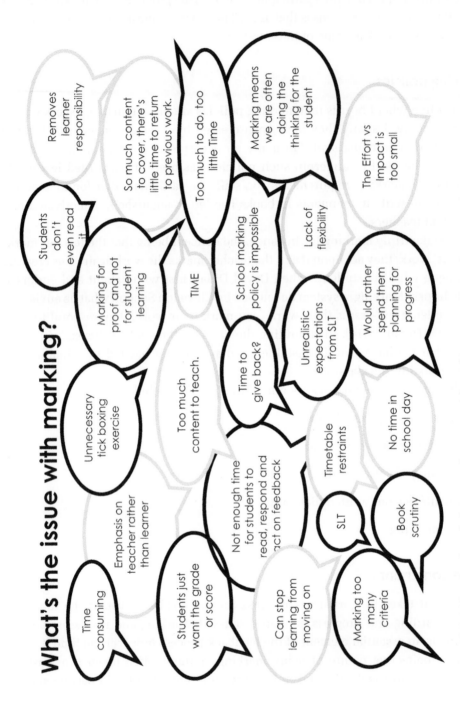

Figure 9.2 What teachers believe are the issues with marking

leaders on average spend eight hours on marking and correcting student work a week (Higton et al., 2017), yet a full-time secondary teacher only receives 10% of their timetabled teaching time for planning, preparation and assessment equating to approximately 2.5 hours a week.

Poor peer assessment

Another issue comes from peer assessment. Often when I rave about peer assessment, I'm met with pessimism. Teachers reel off the mediocre comments they regularly come across such as "well done, your handwriting is pretty", "I liked that you underlined the key word" or even "you got that wrong, try again". None of which are constructive or helpful in pushing forward learning. Yet peer feedback can be a large source of feedback in and out of the classroom.

In fact, Nuthall (2007) notes that 80% of the feedback students receive comes from their peers and whether that be formal or informal, most of it is inaccurate or meaningless. Therefore, if 80% of feedback our students receive comes from their peers, it is essential that we invest in peer assessment to teach and train our students in the art of effective feedback. In doing so, not only do we create feedback masters, specialists in the art or at least competent agents of feedback, but we also create students that are able to develop the capacity to monitor the quality of their own work. Yet if we do not, feedback from peers does little to support progress and learning.

Misunderstanding the role of feedback

For feedback to be truly effective it must work towards closing the gap between what students know, can do and what they understand, with what they need to know, do and understand.

Feedback is just part of the process. The feedback we give and receive during the assessment and marking process should inform our future planning. Formative assessment tells us how effective our teaching has been, how well our students have grasped the content and whether progress is being made over time. For it to be effective, we must use this information to inform our teaching and lesson planning; to reteach if necessary, to adapt our methods, to stretch our students and to close any gaps.

Rather than seeing feedback as a separate entity we must view it as being entwined with instruction. To do so feedback ought to present students with information that specifically relates to the current learning whether it be related to the knowledge or skills being developed. This information should enable students to fill the gap between what has been achieved and what should be achieved; sharing success criteria in advance enables students to self-monitor and make judgements of their work prior to feedback being given.

Scrutiny

Too often than not marking and feedback is used as a way of assessing a teacher's performance and their ability to meet school expectations rather than as a tool to aid learning. The Department for Education's report on *Eliminating unnecessary workload around marking* addresses how marking has become a burden for teachers as frequently it is used to "demonstrate teacher performance or to satisfy the requirements of other, mainly adult, audiences", resulting in the marking itself being monitored rather than the impact that the feedback has on progress and learning.

The use of marking to assess performance and to scrutinise teachers has added excessive pressures on teachers to mark books a particular way and to meet unsustainable objectives. When one of my performance management targets was "*to achieve a minimum of 6 good or outstanding work scrutiny judgements where 1 is to be outstanding across a range of books for the pupils you are responsible for*", I felt a huge amount of pressure to ensure every book was marked up-to-date and in line with the school policy. This meant several hours of marking every evening to ensure this happened, as quite simply I didn't want to disappoint. Unfortunately, I'm not the only one to experience such pressures. I even know of teachers that have been required to deep mark every piece of work or mark books after every lesson; it is simply unsustainable and a major cause of burnout.

What does Ofsted have to say about marking?

In many cases, unsustainable marking practices have been the result of school leaders striving to please Ofsted. The misguided interpretation of Ofsted guidance and inspection reports has often led to imprudent application of what is thought to be regarded as 'good teaching'.

To take steps towards reducing extraneous workload, Ofsted released clarification in their Ofsted Myths guidance as part of the school inspection handbook.

The Ofsted school inspection handbook (2018) states:

- "Ofsted recognises that marking and feedback to pupils, both written and oral, are important aspects of assessment. However, Ofsted **does not** expect to see any specific frequency, type or volume of marking and feedback; these are for the school to decide through its assessment policy. Marking and feedback should be consistent with that policy, which may cater for different subjects and different age groups of pupils in different ways, in order to be effective and efficient in promoting learning.

- While inspectors will consider how written and oral feedback is used to promote learning, Ofsted does not expect to see any written record of oral feedback provided to pupils by teachers".

Ofsted are therefore not expecting to see reams of written dialogue in books, to see work marked every lesson, to see a record of verbal feedback and so on. Therefore, if you are finding school policy dictates strategies that exacerbate workload, you have the power to address it. Speak to your school leaders, give them viable alternatives. Don't be afraid to broach the issue with the senior leadership team. And if they suggest to you that the school policy reflect what Ofsted want to see, direct them to the school inspection handbook with a smile.

And what does research say about marking?

The Education Endowment Foundation report '*A marked improvement? A review of the evidence on written marking*' (Elliott et al. 2016) explores a variety of approaches to marking and feedback. It found that the there are few large-scale, long-term, robust studies on written marking; instead most students have been small scale, over short periods of time. As a result, there is a lack of robust evidence on different forms of written marking. However some common findings have been uncovered, such as that careless errors should be marked differently to errors from misunderstanding, that awarding grades for every piece of work may reduce the impact of marking, that the use of specific and actionable short-term targets are more likely to positively impact progress and that students require some time to consider and respond to marking for it to have influence.

Do we really need to mark books?

Since marking is such a contentious issue at present and there is a lack of long-term evidence as to the effectiveness of marking books, it is difficult to answer the question. What I would say though is that feedback is the important and vital element here, whatever form it takes. Marking in itself provides our students with feedback on their learning and helps teachers to identify misunderstandings. However, this can also be achieved through effective assessment for learning in the classroom and whole-class feedback.

Reducing the workload

Marking and feedback is a necessity of teaching and learning. But it doesn't have to be a burden. The following explores the three pillars of effective marking and feedback, a variety of strategies to implement in your classroom and is followed by how implementing feedback rather than marking polices can help to release the burden.

The three pillars of effective marking (and feedback)

These three pillars were originally suggested by the Department for Education in the "Eliminating unnecessary workload around marking" report published in

March 2016. It was this report that influenced my first presentation on feedback for Pedagoo Hampshire in September 2016 and, later on, my article in the UKEd Magazine in which I discussed my interpretation of the three pillars.

Here's a summary of the three pillars of effective marking (and feedback).

Meaningful

For marking and feedback to be meaningful it needs to be suitable for the age group, and it needs to provide students with something to act upon and delivered within a suitable time frame.

I therefore find it hard to encourage teachers to mark after a set period of time. Feedback needs to be timely to make it meaningful. This doesn't mean marking every piece of work after every lesson, far from it. Instead it's about being selective in deciding what will be formally assessed. This could be an extended piece of writing, an assessment or DME for instance – something that can generally be done over two or more lessons. The marking and feedback gained should then feedforward into future planning to support student progress and provide students with an opportunity to act on feedback given.

Manageable

I'm a firm believer that we as teachers should not have to mark everything in a student's book. I encourage you to review student work with them, glance at it in the lesson and look through books afterwards. But that doesn't mean you need to mark the work. We can gather vital information on progress, understanding and misconceptions without having to write anything in books; instead we can use that information to forward plan and adapt our teaching. There's no need to spend hours writing in books merely to create a visual dialogue between student and teacher.

Like the *Eliminating unnecessary workload around marking* reports says, "if the hours spent do not have the commensurate impact on pupil progress: **stop it**".

Motivating

If marking is to motivate, it requires students to take responsibility of their work.

I rarely provide 'well done, your work is great' kind of comments, my written comments are very much about the achievements and ways to improve for example 'you have effectively backed your explanation up with an example from the text', or 'annotate your diagrams to demonstrate you understand them'. I find that discussing exemplary work has far greater impact on student outcomes than if I were to write a comment of sheer praise in their book.

Additionally, peer assessment when done effectively can exert motivation in students. From experience, I find students are more motivated when their peers are assessing their work, often apologising if their handwriting isn't their neatest or if they've made several spelling mistakes. As we embed peer assessment into the fabric of the classroom, these apologetic comments reduce as students become more self-regulating and check their work themselves before peer assessment takes place.

Finally, marking and feedback has to be motivating for us too. Policies that reduce autonomy and that implicitly increase workload and distract from the planning and delivery of effective lessons simply doesn't have the impact it covets and becomes a burden on teachers and facilitator of burnout. Students should be working harder than the teacher as a result of effective feedback.

Marking and feedback

At my second school, I was developing a department from scratch. It gave me the opportunity to explore assessment strategies, planning and organisation. As you've probably worked out by now, there was a lot of work to be done; but setting up the department gave me the opportunity to trial and implement a variety of workload reducing feedback strategies. I tried and tested a large number until I was able to slim it down to those that worked best for me, my subject area and my students based on John Hattie's 'feed-up, feedback, feedforward' model. These strategies now make up marking and feedback toolkit.

My marking and feedback toolkit

My marking and feedback toolkit strategies are tried and tested, not just in my classroom, but in several classrooms across the country and further afield.

Tool 1: my voice

My most powerful feedback tool is my voice. Before starting an extended piece of work, a project or a summative assessment we feed up by discussing the success criteria, what a good one looks like, what the mark scheme might want from us, what skills will be used etc.

Sometimes we discuss work that has been similar in terms of the skills used and think about the challenges faced and how they could be overcome this time around. We do this verbally, usually discussing in groups, with discussion as a class followed by confirmation from me.

Students then start the work and are provided with verbal feedback as they work through it. This might be from myself or their peers. Usually simple discussions of where the work is going and how it could be improved. It's timely and purposeful. Verbal feedback isn't just given for extended pieces of work but also those little tasks, usually in the form of discussions for clarification.

The last verbal approach is feeding forward, whereby students and I discuss as a class, individually or in groups the successes and potential improvements for future work. Students discuss the challenges they faced and may then make note of their reflections in their books for future reference.

Tool 2: peer assessment

An important element of my toolkit is teaching my classes effective peer assessment. At the start of the school year, I develop the routine with my classes of using a purple pen for peer assessment and pink pen for perfecting the work before submitting as complete. I've trialled a variety of peer assessment strategies with varying degrees of success and found ACE peer assessment most effective.

I usually use ACE feedback whilst students are working on an extended piece of writing or a prolonged task, to allow them to gain feedback and make improvements before they submit their final piece. Yet, it is also an effective tool at the end of a piece of work to help students to set targets for future pieces.

On occasions, I even make use of ACE as part of my feedback routine. In doing so, I simply tick and flick the successes, put a question mark for any mistakes or misconceptions and an asterisk for where the student could extend their work. Sometimes I might either write comments and questions in the book or use whole-class feedback to highlight the successes, errors and how to improve and extend. It works effectively with marking codes and whole-class feedback sheets.

Whilst I highly recommend the ACE strategy it's important you try a range of peer assessment methods to find what works best for you and your context; other peer assessment strategies are described later in this chapter.

ACE Peer Assessment

Accept
Tick the work where you accept what is written. Double tick any particularly good parts.

Challenge
Something doesn't seem right? Challenge it.
Identify with a ◆ and ask a question at the end of the work.

Extend
Does something need more information?
Perhaps some explanation or example is needed? Identify with an * and ask a question or raise a point at the end of the work.

Figure 9.3 Outline of ACE peer assessment

Stop. Peer-Assess. Progress.

Stop what you are doing.

Swap books and peer assess.

Return the book.

Continue with your work.

Make improvements based on the feedback.

THINK PINK, Think Progress.

Figure 9.4 Outline of the stop, peer-assess and progress strategy

Tool 3: Stop. Peer Assess. Progress.

This technique requires students to understand that they should pause, proofread and then continue with their work. I find it helps students to stop making the same reoccurring mistakes such as those associated with spelling, punctuation and grammar as they think hard about what they produce, whilst they also construct higher quality work before submitting for teacher assessment as they are exposed to other examples, collaborative discussion and the opportunity to reflect on progress so far.

Regularly during the task, I will stop my students, usually about half way into the task and get them to peer assess. Students will peer assess in purple pen using the ACE system and write comments or questions at the end or in the margins. Once peer-assessed the work is returned to the student and they act on the feedback there and then in pink pen. Students then continue with the task and each time they make the suggested improvements, anything from the spelling of a key work to the use of data as evidence, they do it in pink to clearly demonstrate the improvements and progress they have made in the remainder of the work.

Tool 4: live marking

This is a game changer. It's diagnostic feedback there and then, when the student needs it. It also influences planning and the direction of learning in a timely fashion. Using an amalgamation of the remaining tools of my kit, I've learnt how to live mark in the classroom as students work, making marking more meaningful, manageable and motivating. And the best thing, live marking doesn't have to written in books; it can be carried out verbally creating a dialogue between student and teacher. I recommend carrying a pen and a highlighter with you as you circulate the classroom to enable you to comment and draw attention to elements of the work that demonstrate successes or offer potential room for improvement.

In carrying out live marking, it reduces the associated workload outside of lessons, gives the teacher feedback on progress and learning and enables a proactive response to short-term lesson planning.

Tool 5: double ticks, successes and next steps

This approach I use for formative assessment throughout the term.

I quite simply use single and double tick to highlight the successes in pieces of work. Double ticks identify to students that these are particularly strong elements of the work. To start with I will justify why the ticks are achieved to the students. As they gain experience in self and peer assessment they then have to explain the double ticks through annotations – this is usually in relation to the skills used within the work such as use of evidence, use of case study facts, stats and specifics and so on, rather than topic specific achievements.

During the live-marking process, I will issue double ticks as I walk around the classroom looking at and discussing work with students. Usually we will verbally discuss why the double tick has been given, and sometimes they may write this down for future reference and reflection.

At the end of a marking session I will provide a brief and concise comment in relation to their successes and next steps. These are often issued through a marking code or a feedback grid, and students are given time to act on the feedback if it requires them to do so. For instance, if I provide them with a question to move

---

The Double Tick

See a double tick?

This identifies a particularly strong aspect of your work.

Annotate in the margin or at the end of your work why you think you received the double tick.

Consider the skills used within the lesson, the piece of work or the focus for our unit of study.

No double tick?

What do you need to do to get one?

Self-assess your work and write a comment at the end on how you could improve it.

Figure 9.5 Outline of how students should engage with the double tick strategy

> **Success and Next Steps**
>
> **Successes**
>
> What have you achieved in your work?
>
> Have you met the success criteria set out before the task?
>
> **Next steps**
>
> What do you need to do to move forward in your work?
>
> What are your next steps?

Figure 9.6 Outline of how students should engage with successes and next steps

their understanding on or to develop an answer they've given, it can be a target they need to focus on in the remainder of the topic, always with the aim to move their learning and progress on.

Tool 6: marking and feedback grids

I use these grids in one of two ways. Firstly, as students work through an extended piece or assessment they are given the feedback grid as an outline of the success criteria they need to meet; as they achieve the criteria it is highlighted, and discussions occur in relation to the next steps that could be taken to improve it. Depending on the age range and ability, sometimes I will write what to do next, highlight next steps on the sheet or give a specific task that will enable the next steps to be achieved.

The second way in which I use them are for the summative assessment of piece of work. I will create the feedback grid as a way of identifying the successes and areas of improvement for the student. Students will read and then reflect upon the feedback to identify their own targets and next steps to focus on through the next topic or piece of work.

Tool 7: Whole-class feedback

Sometimes it is not necessary to write diagnostic comments in student books, particularly in relation to everyday classwork so I use the whole-class feedback approach. On a regular basis, I will take a look through student books and record which students require praise for any particularly outstanding work, any students with unfinished work, any reoccurring misconceptions and SPaG errors and next steps that apply to more than one student on my whole-class feedback record sheet.

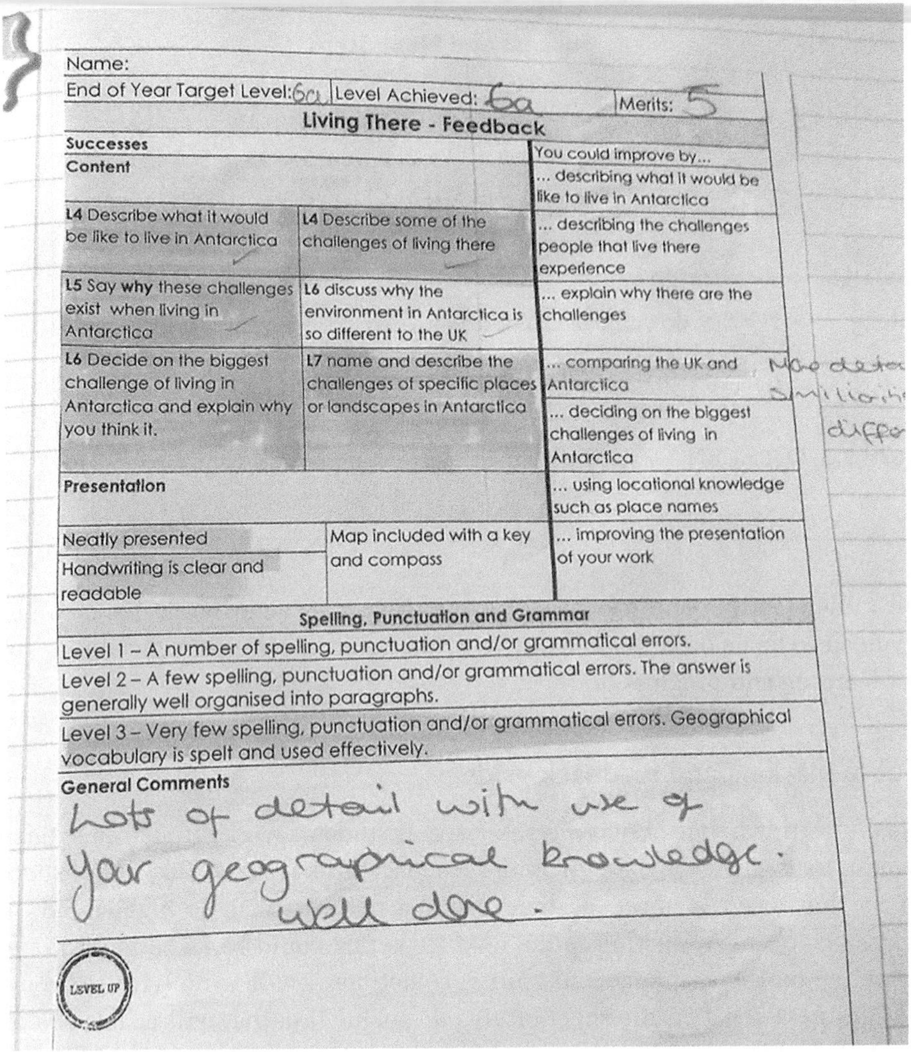

Figure 9.7 Example of a marking grid in use

I then use this information to plan the next sequence of lessons to ensure that misconceptions are dealt with and students have an opportunity to act on the next steps. The whole-class feedback sheet is shared with the students by scanning and projecting it onto the whiteboard. As I explain the elements of the feedback sheet, students write down comments relevant to them. There is more on whole-class feedback later in the chapter.

On my sheet, I have an assessment of understanding section; this bit is not shown to the students. Instead I use it to identify the students I need to work with first or to which I need to apply in-class intervention strategies to ensure their learning moves forward.

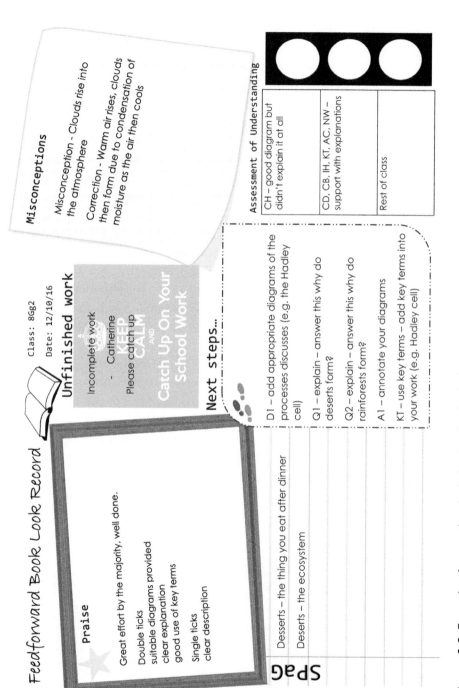

Feedforward Book Look Record

Class: 8g2
Date: 12/10/16

Praise

⭐ Great effort by the majority, well done.

Double ticks
suitable diagrams provided
clear explanation
good use of key terms

Single ticks
clear description

Unfinished work

Incomplete work
  - Catherine

KEEP
CALM
AND
Please catch up
Catch Up On Your
School Work

Misconceptions

Misconception - Clouds rise into the atmosphere

Correction - Warm air rises, clouds then form due to condensation of moisture as the air then cools

Assessment of Understanding

CH – good diagram but didn't explain it at all	○ ○ ○
CD, CB, IH, KT, AC, NW – support with explanations	
Rest of class	

Next steps...

D1 – add appropriate diagrams of the processes discusses (e.g. the Hadley cell)

Q1 – explain – answer this why do deserts form?

Q2 – explain – answer this why do rainforests form?

A1 – annotate your diagrams

KT – use key terms – add key terms into your work (e.g. Hadley cell)

SPaG

Desserts – the thing you eat after dinner

Deserts – the ecosystem

Figure 9.8 Example of a completed whole-class feedback sheet

Tool 8: Feedforward

The final tool of my marking and feedback toolkit is feedforward; using feedback effectively. Feedforward provides constructive guidance on how to improve and the opportunity to do so.

"The learner has to (a) possess a concept of the standard (or goal, or reference level) being aimed for, (b) compare the actual (or current) level of performance with the standard, and (c) engage in appropriate action which leads to some closure of the gap". Sadler, 1989

As many experts will argue, feedback will only benefit learning when it involves students using the feedback in some way. That's not to say that the student must directly engage with the feedback. Instead the teacher can use it to adapt the direction of learning for individuals, groups or the whole class to facilitate action to close the gap.

As a result, a vital element of my classroom practice that is highly influenced by feedback and feedforward is modelling success criteria. As a result of the feedback received from students through assessment of and for learning, I can highlight strengths and struggles in the content covered based upon the experiences of those I previously taught, thus eradicating some of the common errors before they arise. It's a skill that comes with experience, but you shouldn't let that hold you back from modelling success criteria.

Before setting students off onto a task, model it to clarify the goal. This needn't be labour intensive and doesn't require the full process. Demonstrating the method on the whiteboard or using a visualiser is easy to do and can easily be supported with scaffolding strategies.

For example, when I'm teaching students to describe the pattern on a graph, I first introduce an acronym. I like to use GC – general content, SE – specific examples. We discuss what this means, general content being the general pattern evident in the data along with the identification of any anomalies, whilst specific examples

Next steps...	What should I include?	How do I start?
Look at the success criteria that has not been ticked off on your feedback slip. You have 15 minutes to add the criteria to your work. You can rewrite from scratch or add to your original and then extend it.	**Physical Geography** - What physical features does the Middle East have? - Where can these be found?	The Middle East consists of _____ countries including... Some interesting physical features include .... which can be found.... *(use north/south/east/west to describe its location and include the size of the feature)*
Success Criteria [up to 8 possible marks] General location (1) Named at least 3 countries in ME (1) Used directions (1) Named examples of physical features (1) Described where they can be found (2) Described location of major cities (1) Offered reasons for location of major cities (2) S&C – included facts S&C – compared to the UK	**Human Geography** - Where are the big cities located? - Why do you think they are located there?	The major cities in the Middle East include.... I think they might be located here because... *(clue: think about the physical features)*
	Stretch and challenge How does the Middle East compare to the UK?	Comparing the geography of the UK and the Middle East, I think that....

Figure 9.9 Example of feedforward tasks to move students forward

necessitates students to pull out data to support their description. To train them in this I will first go through an example that is not relevant to the content we are studying and will model each stage. Students then try for themselves. If students struggle, scaffolding such as sentence starters or a content tick sheet is put in place to support them.

The benefit of modelling and clarifying the goal is that students can develop an understanding of why they are doing what they are doing and how they are going to achieve it, giving them confidence in the process.

Marking and feedback strategies

I only found what works best through trial, implementation, reflection and amendment. What works for me may not work for you. It is worth trialling a variety of approaches to find what works for you and your context. A primary classroom will require a very different approach to a secondary.

The following are a range of suggestions with explanation of how to implement.

Verbal feedback and live marking

Verbal feedback in my opinion is significantly undervalued and accepted as a form of effective feedback. It's timely, differentiated and allows for immediate action. I've never understood the need to evidence verbal feedback. Why do students need to write down what you said? Why do we have to stamp or write VF in books? Why can't the student just spend the time acting on the feedback given. If they act on it, they are immediately making progress. If they hadn't done a, b and c before your feedback, now they have. . . . That's progress right?

Implementing is easy. Move around the room and mark in-situ through written comments or verbal discussions. Preferably develop dialogue with students through timely conversations that allow for immediate action by the student. There is no requirement from official bodies that states that the provision of verbal feedback necessitates recording; it is far more productive for the student to act on the feedback than to write it down. If you like to write down comments, perhaps use sticky notes to write a brief comment or marking code for students to refer to as they continue to work. Alternatively, live-marking works well with feedback grids outlined next.

Feedback grids

These were the first strategy I implemented on a large scale across all my classes and year groups. They were a time saviour. Not only did they allow me to live mark, they provided students with success criteria. Although they can take some time to create and they require you to clearly know the learning objectives, once implemented they save a great deal of time.

I recommend creating your grids before students undertake an extended piece of work or the topic; you'll know what to expect from your students, and they know too. To live mark, as students work, visit them and discuss what they have achieved so far, tick off or highlight the criteria. Discuss the successes of the work. Follow that up by highlighting through a dot, steps or other way the criteria you want

Name:		
End of Year Target Level:	Level Achieved:	Merits:
Living There - Feedback		
Successes		You could improve by...
Content		... describing what it would be like to live in Antarctica
L4 Describe what it would be like to live in Antarctica	**L4** Describe some of the challenges of living there	... describing the challenges people that live there experience
L5 Say **why** these challenges exist when living in Antarctica	**L6** discuss why the environment in Antarctica is so different to the UK	... explain why there are the challenges
L6 Decide on the biggest challenge of living in Antarctica and explain why you think it.	**L7** name and describe the challenges of specific places or landscapes in Antarctica	... comparing the UK and Antarctica
		... deciding on the biggest challenges of living in Antarctica
Presentation		... using locational knowledge such as place names
Neatly presented. Handwriting is clear and readable	Map included with a key and compass	... improving the presentation of your work
Spelling, Punctuation and Grammar		
Level 1 – A number of spelling, punctuation and/or grammatical errors.		
Level 2 – A few spelling, punctuation and/or grammatical errors. The answer is generally well organised into paragraphs.		
Level 3 – Very few spelling, punctuation and/or grammatical errors. Geographical vocabulary is spelt and used effectively.		
General Comments		
LEVEL UP		

Figure 9.10 Example of a marking and feedback grid for Key Stage 3

them to focus on next and discuss with them how they might approach that. It's at this point you can then determine if they require scaffolding to further progress.

Here's an example . . .

I simply highlight in one colour the achieved criteria and during live marking would put a dot next to the content I wanted them to focus on next. Once the task was complete, I would highlight in another colour the next steps I want them to take and give the students some time to make these improvements in subsequent lessons.

Marking codes

An effective way to provide frequently occurring comments. To deliver this strategy, consider the most common feedback given in your classroom. Create generic feedback statements and give each a simple code. Provide a copy of the code to students and time to act on the feedback.

Humanities Subject Specific

Comments for Targets / Areas to Improve

The following statements will hopefully help you to set meaningful targets and comments for areas to improve within Humanities. There are three approaches you may wish to use:

1. Write the letter and number in the classwork book – display the comments on the board and pupils write down their feedback and respond appropriately during directed improvement and reflection time.

2. Glue a copy of the codes into classwork books at the beginning of the year, write the letter and number in the book as you book. Pupils read the relevant comment and respond during directed improvement and reflection time.

3. Write the whole comment in the pupils book yourself and pupils respond during directed improvement and reflection time.

	KEY
W1 — Use a wider variety of (correctly spelt) key terms more consistently	W – Written work
	S – Skills
W2 — Ensure spelling and punctuation is accurate	G – Geography
W3 — Use a wider variety of descriptive words	H - History
W4 — Develop explanations in your work, using words such as "because"	T – Thinking

---

Figure 9.11 Example of marking codes for Key Stage 3 geography and history

W5 — Use evidence in your writing to support your point

W6 — Make greater reference to graphs, images or other work

W7 — Include more detail in your work

W8 — Ensure your work is well structured, including the use of paragraphs

S1 — Ensure all diagrams, maps or graphs have suitable titles

S2 — Ensure all graph axes are labelled

S3 — Improve the clarity of your graph/diagram work

S4 — Ensure that your graphs have suitable scales

S5 — Accurately plot all points on your graph/diagram

S6 — Ensure that your map work always has a scale, key and compass

S7 — Use 4/6 figure grid references to accurate locate your work

S8 – Use the longitude and latitude to accurately locate places

G1 — Consider scale in your work (local, national, global etc.)

G2 — Consider different viewpoints in your work

G3 — Consider social, economic and environmental categories in your work

G4 — Consider different physical and human processes in your work

G5 — Locate your work, i.e. use latitude, continent, country, distances etc.

G6 — Complete extra research into the topic area to support your enquiry

G7 — Identify different processes and patterns

H1 – Identify primary and secondary sources of information in your work

H2 – Name key historical figures/dates/events in your work

H3 - Demonstrate change and continuity between time periods/events

H4 – Demonstrate cause and consequence in your work

H5 – Consider the importance of historical events

H6 – Assess the reliability/bias of the sources used in your work

H7 – Ask suitable questions about sources and events

T1 — Define the key terminology in your work

T2 — Use greater description in your work

T3— Organise the points in your work – consider the paragraph/sentence structure

T4 — Explain your points with greater detail

T5 — Analyse your work, including looking for patterns and/or correlations

T6 — Justify your opinions using the work you have completed

T7 — Suggest alternatives or different answers to the work completed

T8 — A conclude your work

T9 — Reach judgements in your work

Figure 9.11 (Continued)

1. Question	Mark Scheme	Next steps
2. Describe the distribution of earthquakes. **[3]**	General pattern. Clusters along plate margins. High or low frequencies. Named locations	1A – Give the general pattern as well as specific examples, e.g. the majority of earthquakes are found along the plate boundaries.
Give **two** differences between continental crust and oceanic crust. **[2]**	Continental crust – less dense (about 2.7–2.9 g/cm3), thicker (average between 25 to 70 km), older (oldest being 4.4 billion years old), granite rock. Oceanic crust is denser (3g/cm3), thinner (average between 5–10km), younger, basalt rock.	2A – Don't tell us the obvious.
Give **one** example of a conservative plate margin shown in **Figure 1**. **[1]**	Pacific and North American plate – San Andreas Fault	3A – Review boundary types.
Describe the location of ocean trenches. **[2]**	Destructive margins, ocean-continental plates, found at edge subduction zone where oceanic plate is subducted	4A – Review the difference between an ocean trench (destructive) and a ridge (constructive). 4B – Be more specific with the location (at the end of two plates, above the subduction zone).
With the help of **Figure 1**, outline the differences between constructive and destructive plate margins. **[3]**	Constructive – Plates pulling apart, creates ridges and rift valleys e.g. mid-Atlantic ridge (Eurasian and north American plate). Few earthquakes. destructive – plates push towards one another, creates volcanoes (ocean-continent) and fold mountains (continent – continent). More earthquakes.	5A – Review the difference between the two plate boundaries. 5B – Expand the difference beyond just the movement. 5C – Refer to the figure by giving an example.

Figure 9.12 Example of marking codes in use for GCSE exam style questions

I. Question	Mark Scheme	Next steps
Explain how earthquakes and volcanoes are formed at a destructive plate margin. **[6]**	Movement of plates towards one another due to convection currents. Subduction occurs, slab pull. Magma chamber. Magma rises, erupts through weakness in crust. Over time layers develop with each eruption. Plates moving towards each don't do so smoothly. They get stuck and pressure builds as a result of the friction. When the pressure is suddenly released, seismic waves are produced.	7A – refer to a process, convection or slab pull 7B – use key terminology (subduction) 7C – expand to give full sequence 7D – review earthquakes

Figure 9.12 (Continued)

<u>Peer Assessment Marking Codes</u>

^{SP}
Speeling error which needs correcting.
(Start of sentences need capital letters as
do names of places.
Whilst end of sentences need full stops()
Their going to take there dog over they're.

Figure 9.13 Example of marking codes for peer assessment of spelling, punctuation and grammar

Alternatively, when assessing work produce codes for task specific comments and provide these to students.

Marking codes can also be applied to peer assessment.

Dot marking

There are a variety of ways you can use dot marking. Firstly, you can use it as you live mark; put a dot on the students work where an error or misconception exists. Students then attempts to work it out for themselves or are given verbal guidance from the teacher.

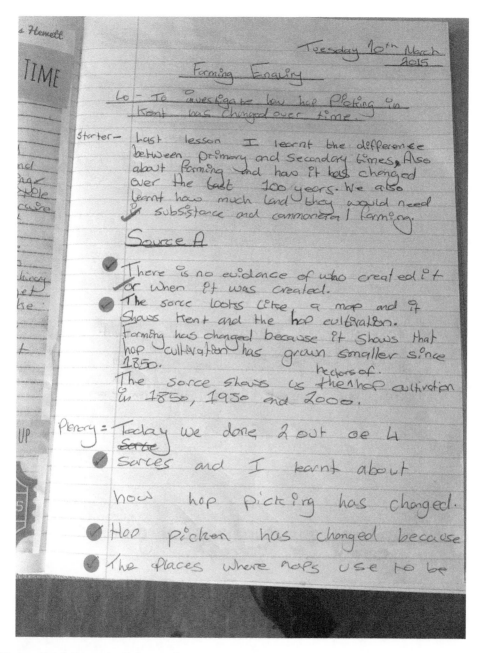

Figure 9.14 Example of dot marking

Dots can be used to indicate where an improvement could be made, followed by time to correct and improve.

Another approach can be that different colour dots indicate different successes or areas for improvement as shown here by Heather James (Tweets as @ LDNHumsTeacher) who discovered the method during one of my workshops.

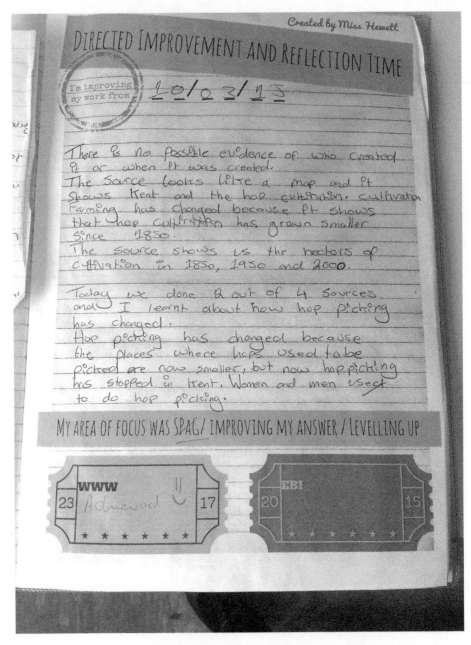

Figure 9.15 Example of improvements made following use of dot marking

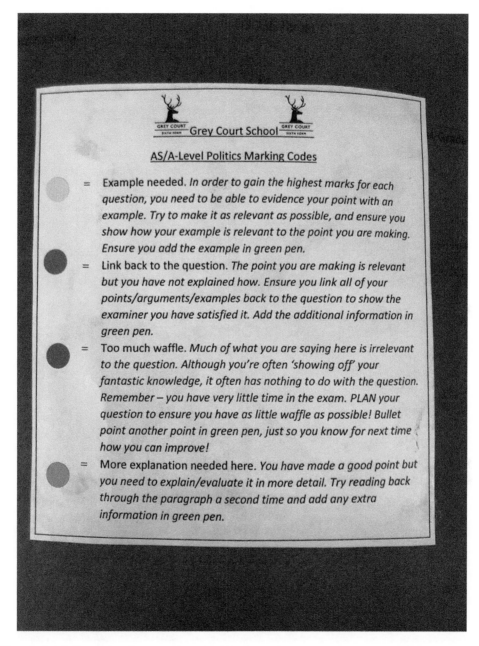

Grey Court School

AS/A-Level Politics Marking Codes

=   Example needed. *In order to gain the highest marks for each question, you need to be able to evidence your point with an example. Try to make it as relevant as possible, and ensure you show how your example is relevant to the point you are making. Ensure you add the example in green pen.*

=   Link back to the question. *The point you are making is relevant but you have not explained how. Ensure you link all of your points/arguments/examples back to the question to show the examiner you have satisfied it. Add the additional information in green pen.*

=   Too much waffle. *Much of what you are saying here is irrelevant to the question. Although you're often 'showing off' your fantastic knowledge, it often has nothing to do with the question. Remember – you have very little time in the exam. PLAN your question to ensure you have as little waffle as possible! Bullet point another point in green pen, just so you know for next time how you can improve!*

=   More explanation needed here. *You have made a good point but you need to explain/evaluate it in more detail. Try reading back through the paragraph a second time and add any extra information in green pen.*

Figure 9.16 Example of dot marking for Key Stage 5 provided by Heather James

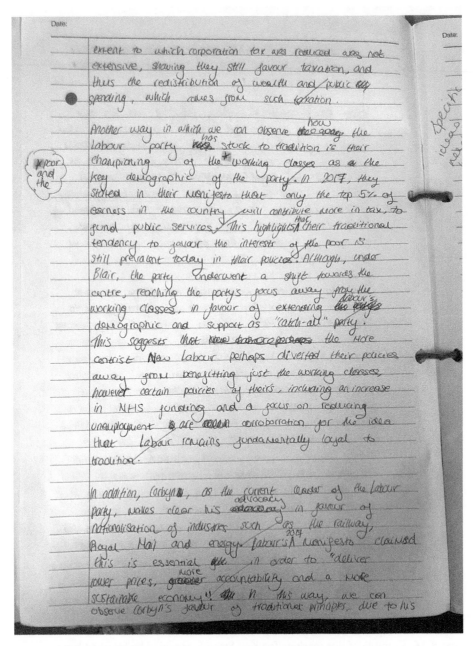

Figure 9.17 Example of dot marking in use provided by Heather James

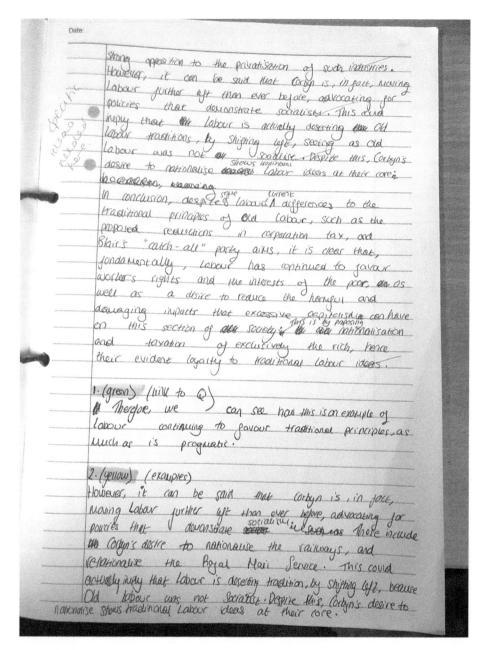

Figure 9.17 (Continued)

Highlight and improve

This technique can be used in isolation or combination with others, notably live marking. It is as simple as it sounds, highlight work that could be improved. You may wish to colour code to specific criteria or provide a brief annotation or verbal comment on how to improve it. It is a useful strategy to encourage students to reflect on their work and determine errors or improvements for themselves.

Highlight and Improve

Has a piece of you work been highlighted?

This means an aspect of your work could be improved.

Either read the comments, listen to the verbal feedback or reflect on the success criteria to work it out.

Act on it in pink pen.

Think Pink. Think Progress.

Figure 9.18 Outline of the highlight and improve strategy

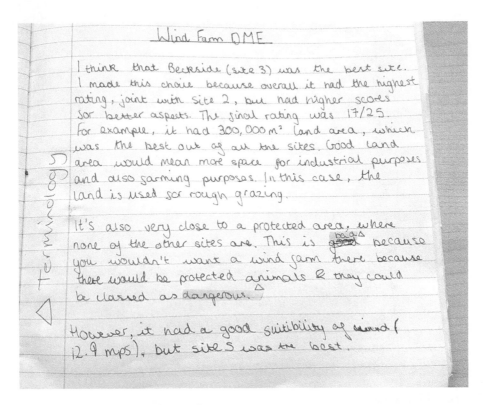

Figure 9.19 Example of highlight and improve in use

Whole-class feedback

Yes, as the name might suggest, feedback is provided to the class as a whole. How you choose to do so will depend on your context. Whole-class feedback usually includes common errors and/or misconceptions, frequent spelling mistakes and the recurrent successes. You may wish to include specific examples of excellence.

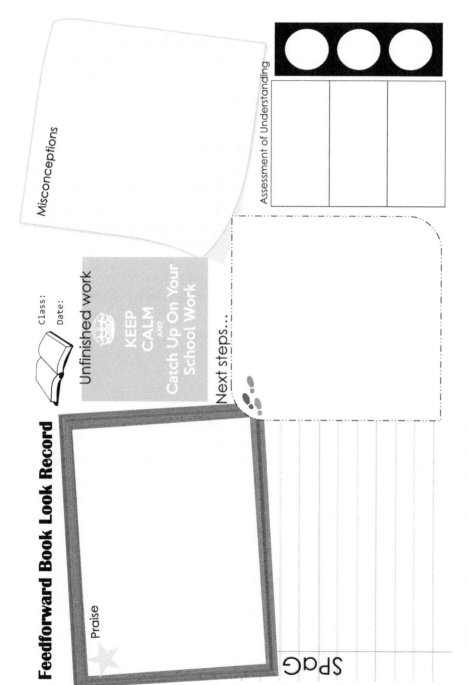

Figure 9.20 Example of a whole-class feedback sheet template

However, aim to have students act on or make use of specific feedback shared with the class in a timely manner.

Here are a few suggestions for using whole-class feedback

■ WCF sheet. Fill in the sheet as you review students work. You may wish to combine it with a marking code and record the codes on the work to identify individual successes and next steps. You may wish to give students an individual copy of the whole-class feedback sheet and have them highlight the content relevant to them. Alternatively, students may be required to write relevant comments into their books.

■ Display and discuss. In this method of WCF the teacher simply verbalises the feedback to the students as they go through an example or mark scheme. As they do so, students annotate their work with the relevant feedback.

■ What a good one looks like. Along with the feedback on WCF sheet, the teacher shares an exemplar of good practice to help students to develop and improve their own work.

The benefit of whole-class feedback is that not only does it provide feedback to students, for the teacher formative assessment can take place in a very short period time, supporting planning and identification of where to direct support, where to scaffold and where to employ intervention strategies.

Word of caution

Don't expect students to be able to identify the information relevant to them to begin with. Training students to understand and make use of whole-class feedback is a necessity. I suggest scaffolding students in the initial stages of identifying relevant feedback and how they can improve by using their names on the sheet or marking codes in their books; for younger year groups, it maybe that the use of codes continues to maintain direction towards relevant feedback.

Self and peer assessment strategies

The opportunity to peer assess I feel isn't just about the outcome (comments, grade, marks, levels etc.) but about the process as a whole. Students see other work of varying degrees of quality allowing reflection upon what they see. It's an opportunity for idea sharing and sparking inspiration. A time to reflect on one's own strengths and weaknesses. A chance to consider successes and areas for improvement. An opportunity to gain feedback before submitting work. Personally, I believe peer assessment is more than just about the feedback, it's a learning experience and should be planned and incorporated into lesson plans.

SpACE Peer Assessment

Spellings

Check the work for spelling mistakes, highlight with Sp.

Accept

Tick the work where you accept what is written. Double tick any particularly good parts.

Challenge

Something doesn't seem right? Challenge it.

Identify with a ❤ and ask a question at the end of the work.

Extend

Does something need more information?

Perhaps some explanation or example is needed? Identify with an * and ask a question or raise a point at the end of the work.

Act on the feedback in pink pen.

Think Pink. Think Progress.

Figure 9.21 Outline of SpACE peer assessment

SpACE

An extension of my ACE peer assessment strategy, adapted by Kim Constable who tweets and blogs as @HecticTeacher. In addition to the accept, challenge and extend, students also assess spelling, punctuation and grammar.

Kind, Specific, Helpful

Students feedback using kind, specific and helpful comments. To support students, you may wish to provide students with sentence stems such as those below.

Kind Sentence Stems

I really enjoyed . . .

I like the way you have . . .

The most successful element was . . .

I thought it was effective when you . . .

Specific Sentence Stems

You might want to think about changing/adding . . .

Add more detail to . . .

You could develop . . .

It didn't quite make sense when you said . . .

Helpful

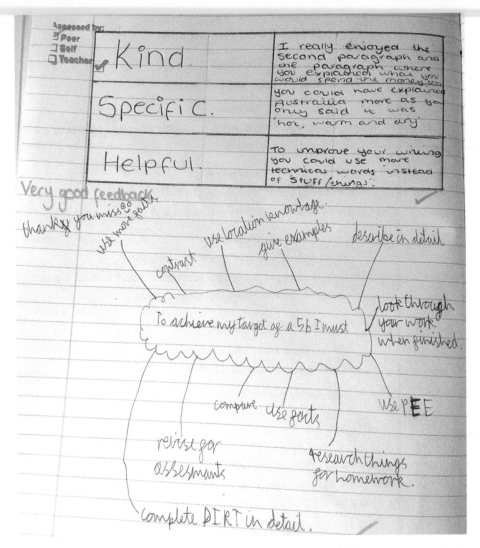

Figure 9.22 Example of kind, specific and helpful feedback in use

To improve the paragraph on. . .
Add an example to. . .
Develop your point on. . .
Change the bit where you said. . .

Keep, bin, build

A nice simple strategy that involves redrafting. During peer assessment students highlight 'Keep' content that meets the criteria for the task, 'bin' content that does not meet the criteria and will not be needed, whilst 'build' content indicates elements that students should expand during the redraft process.

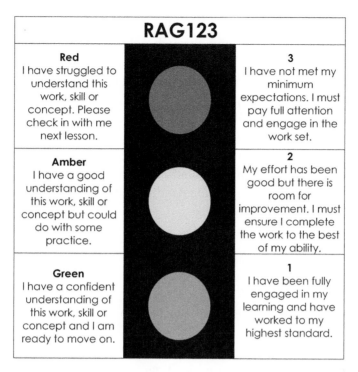

Figure 9.23 Outline of criteria for RAG123

RAG123

A very simple way of the teacher gaining feedback on student's confidence in what they have covered whilst also encouraging student responsibility through the assessment of their effort. With RAG123, students identify where their understanding is on a traffic light RAG scale and where they place their effort on a 1 to 3 scale. Although it doesn't give the teacher feedback on what they know, it helps in identifying where to direct support in the following lesson.

Moving from marking to feedback

Since my first presentation on the 'Less is More: Marking with Purpose' at Pedagoo Hampshire in September 2016, I've become a huge advocate of feedback not marking policies.

The Eliminating unnecessary workload around marking report (2016) from the Department for Education clearly recognises the negative impact high quantity written feedback is having on teachers and the limited impact on student progress. Yet still for many marking policies require an unnecessary frequency and depth of marking, that ultimately creates an unmanageable workload.

The *Eliminating unnecessary workload around marking* report clearly states that "no Government or Ofsted guidance or policy has set deep marking as a requirement. The Teachers' Standards state that teachers should 'give pupils regular feedback, both orally and through accurate marking, and encourage pupils to respond to the feedback". This is not a requirement for pupils to provide a written response to feedback" meaning that it should be that students act on the feedback in subsequent work (Department for Education, 2016). So why are so many school still insisting a written dialogue and regular deep marking?

To move from marking policies to feedback policies it requires whole-school input, development and implementation. Changing parental and student perceptions of marking and their understanding of feedback is also necessary as is highlighting forms of hidden feedback.

An effective feedback policy should

▪ Appreciate the value of verbal feedback

▪ Identify forms of hidden feedback

▪ Give greater autonomy to individual teachers and departments

▪ Reduce marking

▪ Support short-term and long-term planning

▪ Meet the needs of learners

▪ Promote self and peer assessment

▪ Embed assessment for learning

▪ Accept that feedback and student action may not be visibly evident in books

For a range of marking and feedback templates visit www.mrshumanities.com/feedbacktemplates

Snippets of insight

"Feedback and marking is necessary, teachers just need more time to do it. For example, one of the main workload pressures if you teach exam classes is marking formal internal assessments such as mock exams. For just one GCSE class this can be 200 maths papers a year – it's really time consuming but necessary. We just need to be given time to do it". *Jo Morgan, Maths Lead Practitioner, Harris Federation and UK Blog Award Winner 2017. Tweets as @mathsjem*

"Whole class feedback provides insight for the teacher on what the students have grasped whilst providing students with the feedback they need to improve. It is much less time consuming than long written comments on every student's work with clear impact on progress". *Rebecca Foster, Head of English. Tweets as @TLPMsF*

"The strategies I find most effective are pre-printed sheets that I can highlight the key points on and ongoing verbal dialogue with students. Not everything needs to be marked or to a prescribed policy, teachers should be allowed and trusted to give feedback how they see fit". *Gill Rowland, Senior Lecturer at Canterbury Christ Church University. Tweets as @gillrowland1*

"Where possible, circulate as part of the task and assess in the lesson. Develop quality self and peer assessment based on precise criteria and only deep mark specific tasks. Have a marking timetable (and stick to it!)". *Ed Brodhurst, Assistant Headteacher. Tweets as @brodhurst*

"The most effective strategy I've implemented is the whole class feedback sheet- courtesy of Mrs Humanities! I fill these out as I look over a specific piece of work only. For example, those that have produced a good piece of work (and what exactly they did well), those that need to improve (and what they need to do), common misconceptions and SPAG. I upload a copy, have it on the screen as I give verbal feedback next lesson, and DIRT can then follow. I also find the use of model answers effective – either before attempting a task in class (where I might use a model answer on a totally different topic but containing the same expected elements) or writing out a model answer (live modelling) in front of the class whilst talking them through my thought process, after the class have attempted their own first. Again, DIRT can follow this". *Sarah Larsen, Teacher of Geography. Tweets as @sarahlarsen74*

"Verbal feedback given during the lesson is the most effective strategy in my opinion. It's live, children can respond to it there and then, and you can see straight away if they have understood the feedback and acted upon it. No different coloured pens needed, no long comments that rarely get read necessary, no need to sit for hours afterwards marking loads of books". *Adrian Bethune, Teacher and author of 'Wellbeing in the Primary Classroom: A Practical Guide to Teaching Happiness'. Tweets as @AdrianBethune*

Takeaways

- All marking is feedback but not all feedback is marking.

- Embrace variety in how you give feedback.

- Try different strategies to find what works for you and your context.

- Less is more; extensive written dialogue doesn't necessarily lead to progress.

- Students need the opportunity to act on feedback for it to impact learning.

- Feedback should influence short and long-term planning.

References

Elliott, V., Baird, J., Hopfenbeck, T.N., Ingram, J., Thompson, I., Usher, N., Zantout, M., Richardson, J. & Coleman, R. (2016) *A marked improvement? A review of the evidence on written marking* [Online] Available at https://educationendowmentfoundation.org.uk/public/files/Publications/EEF_Marking_Review_April_2016.pdf [Accessed 17th August 2018]

Education Endowment Foundation (2018) *Teaching and learning toolkit* [Online] Available at https://educationendowmentfoundation.org.uk/evidence-summaries/teaching-learning-toolkit/ [Accessed 17th August 2018]

Department for Education (2016) *Eliminating unnecessary workload around marking* [Online] Available at www.gov.uk/government/publications/reducing-teacher-workload-marking-policy-review-group-report [Accessed 3rd March 2018]

Didau, D. (2014) *Why 'triple marking' is wrong (and not my fault)* [Online] Available at https://learningspy.co.uk/leadership/triple-marking-wrong-not-fault-2/ [Accessed 17th August 2018]

Hattie, J., & Timperley, H. (2007) The Power of Feedback. *Review of Educational Research*, 77(1), 81–112.

Higton, J. et al. (2017) *Teacher workload survey 2016 research report February 2017* [pdf] Department for Education. Available at www.isc.co.uk/media/4410/tws_2016_final_research_report_feb_2017.pdf [Accessed 3rd March 2018]

McCallum, D. (2016) *The Feedback-Friendly Classroom: How to Equip Students to Give, Receive, and Seek Quality Feedback That Will Support Their Social, Academic, and Developmental Needs.* Pembroke Publishers, Ontario, Canada

Nuthall, G. (2007) *The Hidden Lives of Learners.* New Zealand Council for Educational Research. Wellington, New Zealand

Ofsted (2018) *Ofsted school inspection handbook, handbook for inspecting schools in England under section 5 of the education act 2005* [pdf] Available at https://assets.publishing.service.gov.uk/government/uploads/system/uploads/attachment_data/file/730127/School_inspection_handbook_section_5_270718.pdf [Accessed 26th October 2018]

Sadler, D. R. (1989) Formative Assessment and the Design of Instructional Systems. *Instructional Science*, 18(2), 119–144.

10 Work-life balance – less is more

Teaching is a career whereby the job could take over your life. There is always something more that could be done; whether it comes from the Government, local authority, senior leaders, middle leaders or ourselves. We want the best for our students; we want them to learn, progress and achieve. Why else would we do this job?

Yet we need to recognise and remember that teaching is a job, not a lifestyle. We need to stand up for our profession, our mental health and our wellbeing. This must be done by us, both as individuals and as a professional body.

First off, we need to understand the impact our work has on our physical and mental health. Each of us can tolerate different levels of stress. We each approach our wellbeing differently, and we all have variations to what it means to have a work-life balance. Yet we all have a set of similar reactions which is why it is vital we understand the signs and symptoms of occupational burnout to ensure we look after ourselves and our colleagues.

Secondly, we need to understand what positive wellbeing looks like for us as individuals and what a work-life balance should consist of as a profession. From there we can plan how we manage our individual wellbeing, workload and pressures of the job, whilst fighting to improve the work-life balance for all teachers and school leaders.

Understanding teacher burnout

The truth be told, I didn't realise how burnout I'd become until I reached breaking point. Even then I didn't realise how bad burnout I had been until almost twelve months later when I'd finally come to terms with the events of the previous school year.

It was almost a year after my breakdown that I found a photo of myself, a photo from April 2016. It was heart wrenching to see it. Puffy eyes, skin drained of colour, hair wispy and nest like. I didn't know that this was what I had come to look like. My families concern all started to make sense. It was clearly more than just a bit of stress I'd been experiencing.

When I found the photo, it made me recall the tears and the constant emotional rollercoaster I had been on; the sense of disdain I felt for the job; the persistent panic before briefings; the frustration and longing to be elsewhere; the panic attacks.

The most saddening thing for me is that I haven't a unique story. There are many teachers out there both within the UK and further afield having experienced or currently experiencing similar or even worse.

In the UK, the Health and Safety Executive reported in 2017, that in the teaching profession alone some '1,860 cases per 100,000 workers' were reported to have experienced work-related stress in a twelve-month period over 2016– 2017 – and that's just those that reported it. The Education Support Partnership's teacher wellbeing index 2018 revealed that "67% of education professional described themselves as stressed at work" with those working in secondary schools reporting higher levels of stress. This stress has a knock-on effect on our ability to perform at work and ultimately, whether directly or indirectly, on student outcomes.

What is occupational burnout?

Occupational burnout is considered to be the result of long-term work-related stress that leads to exhaustion and the inability to function effectively with an array of mental, physical and behavioural characteristics. Yet there is a significant difference between general work stress and burnout, the difference being our ability to recover and return to normal conditions one week to the next.

Initially the term 'burnout' was coined by the American psychologist Herbert Freudenberger in the 1970's as a consequence of severe stress and high morals in professions whereby the worker would sacrifice themselves for the good of others, which he described as "the dedicated and committed" (Freudenberger, 1974, p. 161). He described the mental and physical state of burnout as being "exhausted by making excessive demands on energy, strength or resources' in the workplace" (Freudenberger, 1974, p. 159), thus putting teachers and education staff at high risk due to the caring and social nature of the profession. It's no wonder that as accountability pressures, workload and hours increase whilst pay remains low in comparison to other graduate roles, and that burnout is so high within schools.

Since then a great deal of research has gone into the concept of burnout, with the Maslach Burnout Inventory being created to measure the degree of burnout present. Despite this there is still a lot to be done to reduce occupational burnout in teaching.

Identifying occupational burnout

Firstly, burnout is considered to have a wide range of symptoms. Generally there's a lack of general agreement of all those symptoms but there are three main symptoms that are considered to be a sign of the condition.

1   Exhaustion
    For teachers, this may include both emotional and physical exhaustion. Evidence of this maybe frustration and being irritability, mood swings, impaired concentration, chronic fatigue and insomnia as well as physical symptoms such as increased illness, palpitations, gastrointestinal pain, headaches and dizziness.

2   Depersonalisation
    For teachers, this may develop through cynicism and detachment. Evidence of this maybe pessimism towards teaching, students, colleagues or the school itself, a lack of contact and involvement with others, increasing isolation or a loss of enjoyment from the things that once brought pleasure.

3   Reduced performance
    For teachers, this may develop through negative feelings, lack of productivity and poor performance. Evidence of this maybe feelings of hopelessness and apathy, low self-confidence, increased irritability with one's self and others, increased time spent completing tasks and apathy to want to do so.

If you're feeling like you may be on the road to burnout, do not fear. There's plenty of help and support out there. If you're based in the UK I highly recommend speaking to the Education Support Partnership on their freephone number 08000 562 561 or visiting their website at www.educationsupportpartnership.org.uk for more information.

There are plenty of online tools and websites to make use of if you're experiencing stress or facing burnout such as www.mindtools.com and www.mind.org.uk.

Relationship between burnout and depression

Being able to identify burnout is important to reduce its impact on your physical and mental health; I say this from experience. After I reached breaking point and couldn't continue anymore, I finally accepted I was also suffering from depression and had been for a while.

"Depression is a common mental disorder that causes people to experience depressed mood, loss of interest or pleasure, feelings of guilt or low self-worth,

disturbed sleep or appetite, low energy, and poor concentration". Mental Health Foundation, 2018

I finally went to the doctors for help after speaking to the Education Support Partnership. I didn't know what I wanted from the doctor, but the doctor listened, and from there they offered suggestions. I opted for medication in the form of anti-depressants and some time off work.

I started taking medication immediately. Initially the first prescription didn't work; it made me feel suicidal. I returned to the doctors and had the medication changed. These tablets were effective at giving me the mental space to start to think more clearly. I remained on those tablets over two years. It is only now, as I write this that I am finally coming off the tablets.

At first, I felt ashamed for being on anti-depressants, then when they started to work I realised I hadn't been able to think this clearly for years. Since I started my teaching career I hadn't been able to go to work without a sinking feeling in the pit of my stomach; I hadn't been able to do non-school related activities without the teacher guilt; I hadn't been able to put myself first before my job. Now it felt like I had a mental freedom from constant anxiety.

With the mental freedom, came finding strategies to manage my thoughts, manage my anxieties and manage my workload.

I recognise that medication isn't for everyone, but help comes in many forms. You'll need to be willing and brave enough to go and find it. If you feel you may need support now or in the future, here are some suggestions to get you started

- Speak to a GP.

- Contact a helpline.

- Contact an online or phone-based counselling service.

- Organise counselling sessions.

- Try Cognitive Behavioural Therapy.

- Try talking therapies.

- Speak to family and friends.

- Try a variety of support strategies.

- Try medication, don't fear changing if the first doesn't work for you.

With stress, burnout and negative mental health experiences on the rise in teaching it's important we work together to bring about change to reduce stress and to improve our work-life balance. In doing so we improve the wellbeing of our profession, leading to happier schools.

Understanding wellbeing

Figure 10.1 Wellbeing quote

What is wellbeing?

Gillett-Swan and Sargeant (2014) defined wellbeing as "an individual's capacity to manage over time, the range of inputs, both constructive and undesirable that can, in isolation, affect a person's emotional, physical and cognitive state in response to a given context".

It is quite clear therefore that any teacher with poor wellbeing and experiencing high levels of stress associated with work will not be able to perform to the best of their ability, and that this will negatively impact on the outcomes of students.

Stress can impact energy levels, cognitive ability, patience, mood and so on. The accumulation of such can lead to burnout and absence. Yet a teacher with high satisfaction, wellbeing and low stress will ultimately perform better. Why then is staff wellbeing not a priority for many schools in the UK?

Research from the UK, USA and Australia all demonstrate how stress and poor work-life balance has impacted the wellbeing of teachers in recent years; the UK is not alone in the issue. The announcement from the Department for Education to tackle workload and improve wellbeing was a welcomed message but still it needs to filter into many schools across the UK.

What does positive wellbeing look like?

We all have our own versions of what wellbeing means for us, which is why I have such an issue with wellbeing days and events for staff as part of directed time.

I have a big problem with so-called 'wellbeing days' for staff. Certainly, many of us may enjoy the rural walk, the head massage and the yoga session. But to be forced to partake in such activities during directed time, I feel hinders the point of improving staff wellbeing.

Staff wellbeing comes from active engagement in reducing workload, improving the balance and ensuring staff have the choice to decide how they spend their free time whether it be on their own or with family and friends, being active or enjoying downtime reading fiction.

Wellbeing is personal. How individuals embed a sense of wellbeing into their lives is up to them so long as it makes them happy, positive and feeling rested from the endeavours of the day-to-day of the job.

Opportunity to think

What makes you happy?

What would you consider a good work-life balance?

How can you maximise the time you have available?

Taking charge of your wellbeing

As teachers, we must remember that we are only human. There is only so much we can do in the time we have. We need to balance both our work and our own lives whilst also fitting in some rest and relaxation.

With all the pressures from above as well as our own personal desires to succeed, we need to ensure we take charge of our *own* wellbeing and maintain a work-life balance. Whilst others can support it, we are the only ones that can change it.

You'll need persistence and courage; you'll have to be downright stubborn at times but in the end, it pays off. Your students still learn, progress and succeed; but you will have relaxed, taken time for yourself and enjoyed life.

Every one of us will have a different version of what it means to have good wellbeing, to have a happy work-life balance; but we all have common ground in how we can achieve it.

Top tips to take charge

1 Learn to say no

Possibly one of the hardest things I've learnt to do is say no to myself and others. As much as you might not want to say no, learning to say it is vital for your own sanity, health and wellbeing. Generally speaking, teachers want to do the best for their students, they also want to be good at what they do. That means we sometimes take on far more than we should. Before my breakdown, I struggled with saying no. Partly due to my desire to succeed, but also partly due to the performance management process. I did everything I thought I had to do to succeed; yet too much of that work had little impact on student outcomes. I've learnt now to question requests and tasks to consider the benefit to my students versus the time taken to achieve. As a result, I say no a lot more both to myself and others.

2 Prioritise

Knowing what you value in life will help you to distinguish how you wish to use your time. Don't feel like you have to plan out your time meticulously but know for instance that you want to be around to feed, bath and read to your children at the end of the day means you can plan your time. Work around your priorities, don't let your priorities fit around your work. The marking can wait; the lesson planning can too. You might pass a book scrutiny, but life will pass you by.

3 Be Proactive

Be determined to improve your situation. Discuss wellbeing and work-life balance with the optimism that it can be achieved. Suggest and promote solutions to reduce workload. Know what you want and work for it; we can't just expect that someone else will do something to reduce our workload.

4 Manage your time

Organise how you will spend you working time such as during PPAs, before or after school. Have a clear vision as to what you want to achieve. Set time frames and stick to them. Remember that less is more.

5 Say thank you

This may sound like an odd one, but I've found saying thank you and showing appreciation for the things others do helps me to feel happier and more positive. As a society, we find it a lot easier to be critical than we do to be grateful and appreciative. Yet there are a number of studies on the benefits of gratitude on mental health. There are so many ways to show someone your appreciation from gift giving to making a cup of tea. Whatever you do, share and appreciate the moment.

Teacher5aday

Becoming involved with the teacher5aday movement was a game changer for me. It gave me confidence in finding time for me and a support network I would never have imagined having.

I first became involved in the Teacher5aday movement when I saw a tweet from Martyn Reah, a Deputy Head and geography teacher, who in December 2014 introduced the world to the Teacher5aday concept. Since then it has become a movement of its own and pushed the agenda for positive wellbeing for all teachers and school staff.

Teacher5aday started with Martyn launching the movement at a TeachMeet in December 2014. It was then followed by a plea for wellbeing pledges for the month of January to get us looking after and putting ourselves first for a change. From then on, the hashtag was born, #Teacher5aday, if you haven't looked it up already go and do so now.

Instantly I knew this was for me. 30 December 2014, I published my first involvement with Teacher5aday, and whilst I haven't lived by it day-to-day, it has helped me to find time for me during the busy school day.

How does Teacher5aday work?

Teacher5aday originates from a framework developed by the John Muir Trust and research from the New Economics Foundation (NEF) Centre for Wellbeing. It involves participants considering and taking action under five umbrella concepts: connect, be active, take notice, keep learning and give. Each umbrella has a hashtag associated to help participants to find ideas and see what others are doing. There's a whole heap of participants on Twitter, I highly recommend checking the hashtag out #teacher5aday.

The 5 umbrella concepts

Connect   #connect

Participants concern themselves with taking action to connect with others, or even themselves.

Suggestions:

- Collaborate with other teachers, staff or schools.

- Attend social and academic events.

- Set up or attend a club in or outside of school.

- Meditate or practice mindfulness.

- Phone a friend or family member that you haven't spoken to for a while.

Be active   #exercise

Participants undertake exercise or general activity to be more active.

Suggestions:

- Take a stroll during a school break, before or after school.

- Explore your local area or school grounds.

- Join a gym, sports club or sign up to an exercise class.

- Start an exercise or sports club for school staff.

- Join in with other participants in #OutRunMay.

Take Notice #Notice

Participants concentrate on the world around them, reflecting on experiences and appreciating them.

Suggestions:

- Take photos of natural and man-made beauty.

- Keep a journal.

- Create a scrapbook or physical photo album.

- Go on a notice walk, look for specific things such as letters in nature or oddities.

- Keep a gratitude list.

Keep Learning #Learn

Participants continue to learn; whether something new or an old interest.

Suggestions:

- Read non-fiction books of interest.

- Attend a conference or lecture.

- Try a new craft.

- Write a poem or story.

- Learn how to set up a blog.

Give #Volunteer

Participants strive do something nice for others by volunteering their time and effort, whether big or small.

Suggestions:

- Volunteer in the local community.

- Create a wellbeing space or scheme in your school.

- Take part in a beach clean or other litter picking activity.

- Offer to teach somebody one of your skills.

- Join the Teacher5aday Buddy Box scheme (shameless plug) and become a wellbeing buddy for somebody.

Ideally like with recommendations for fruit and veg, we do one action for each umbrella concept each day. They can be as big or small an action as you like.

I found that when I started doing small things like spending one small moment looking at the view before getting out of the car in the morning or going outside for a breath of fresh air at break, it became easier to say yes to do bigger actions like taking an entire evening off from doing work. Although it would be sometime before the teacher guilt would waver, it gave me the confidence to start putting myself first with the knowledge that others were doing the same.

Teacher5aday has now grown into a movement with themes taking place throughout the year such as #21daysJuly or #FitFeb and events such as annual August slow chat. As well as that, it has inspired offshoot projects such as the teacher5aday journal and buddy box scheme, my favourite being Martyn's Pedagoo Hampshire event, with a focus on creating wellbeing in schools.

Visit Martyn's blog for more information on Teacher5aday http://martynreah. wordpress.com

The Teacher5aday movement also inspired me to set up Teacher5aday Buddy Box in February 2016, which now has over 2000 participants from the UK and beyond. The idea is simple; participants sign up and wait for their buddy's details to arrive by email. Once connected, participants agree to send each other up to four boxes full to the brim with wellbeing treats throughout the school year. The result has been blossoming friendships, wellbeing boosts and many happy recipients.

For more information visit www.teacher5adaybuddybox.com.

Support for education staff

Education Support Partnership
  UK-wide: **08000 562 561**
  Text: **07909 341229**
  What services do they offer over the phone?
  Emotional Support (Counselling)
  Action Plan Support (Coaching)
  Referral service (Information and signposting)

Snippets of insight

There is only so much insight I can give when it comes to looking after your wellbeing; we all need something different. And to be honest, it's not until

Figure 10.2 Example of Teacher5aday Buddy Boxes sent and received

experiencing a breakdown that I've become very good at it. To help here are some very valuable suggestions from eduTwitter colleagues.

"Take a couple of ten-minute walks outside throughout the day. Have certain friends you never talk about teaching with". *Rufus Johnstone, Lead Coach. Tweets as @rufuswilliam*

"Have a buddy. One in SLT helps. SLT aren't monsters though some need to think about the image they convey. Trust is important". Andrew Cowley, Deputy Headteacher and author of 'The Wellbeing Toolkit'. Tweets as @andrew_cowley23

"Ring-fence time for yourself where you will do no work. Work, like a gas, will expand to fill the time you give it so accept you'll never feel 'finished' but you do need to have time for yourself and for your friends/family. No matter what the pressures from work are, that time needs to be protected. You may even find that you work more efficiently because you're giving work less time and you feel more refreshed and energised from giving yourself a well-deserved break". *Rebecca Foster, Head of English. Tweets as @TLPMsF*

"Talk: never hold in things that trouble or worry you. Don't side line family, friend or me time". *Gill Rowland, Senior Lecturer at Canterbury Christ Church University. Tweets as @gillrowland1*

"Engage and appreciate. Go and see people to say thank you; I loved what you did; your students said; a parent called to say; are you ok? and if you're a leader in any form ask what can I do? A nice hand-written card to notice what people do is worth a stack. Bottom line – your time is the most precious currency you'll ever have. Give it out". *Ed Brodhurst, Assistant Headteacher. Tweets as @brodhurst*

"Get to bed on time! A good night's sleep can mean the difference between me being absolutely on fire in the classroom and the lesson going to pot! Tiredness and stress can affect the vocal chords – your voice is your most precious tool, so look after it by looking after yourself! Plan something you enjoy at the weekend or one evening, no matter how small. For example, meeting with a friend, watching a film or going for a run". *Sarah Larsen, Teacher of Geography. Tweets as @sarahlarsen74*

"Keep things in perspective – teaching is not a life and death profession (emergency medicine is!) even though pressure can make it feel like it is. It's important but it's not the most important job in the world. Do the best you can but remember that at the end of the day, the sun is still shining, the world is still spinning, life goes on". *Adrian Bethune, Teacher and author of 'Wellbeing in the Primary Classroom – A Practical Guide to Teaching Happiness'. Tweets as @AdrianBethune*

"Put yourself first. This is something that teachers seem to find really difficult, and it's frighteningly easy to be so busy you can't see that your wellbeing is suffering. Check in with yourself and see how you are feeling. Be kind to yourself, you are no good to anyone, especially your pupils, if you are exhausted. Don't feel like you have to be Pinterest perfect all the time, no one else is, no matter how it may look from the outside. Do what makes you happy as much as you can. If your work is regularly compromising your ability to do this, it's time to look for a move". *Sam Collins, Founder of Schoolwell. Tweets at @samschoolstuff*

Takeaways

- Make time for yourself each week.

- Work will always be there, but you must be strict on how much you do outside of directed time.

- Look out for the signs of burnout in yourself and colleagues.

- Say no when you need to, to both yourself and others.

References

Freudenberger, H. (1974) Staff Burnout. *Journal of Social Issues*, 30, 159–165.

Gillett-Swan, J. K., & Sargeant, J. (2014) Wellbeing as a Process of Accrual: Beyond Subjectivity and Beyond the Moment. *Social Indicators Research*, 121(1), 135–148.

Health and Safety Executive (2017) *Work-related stress, depression or anxiety statistics in Great Britain 2017* [pdf] Available at www.hse.gov.uk/statistics/causdis/stress/stress.pdf [Accessed 27th October 2018]

Mental Health Foundation (2018) *Depression* [Online] Available at www.mentalhealth.org.uk/a-to-z/d/depression [Accessed 27th October 2018]

Thriving

Despite what you might hear, it is possible to find ways to not just survive in teaching but to thrive as well. Now that I've found the right school, I feel like a person again and not just the embodiment of a 'teacher'. It may take some time as pedagogy is developed, workload reducing techniques trialled and you get to grips with what you are doing; but patience and determination will help. In the following pages, we will explore how to go beyond surviving and how to thrive in this rewarding profession.

The following chapters will discuss the importance of developing subject knowledge and how to develop it with as small a burden on your time as possible. We will consider how taking on responsibility may impact your workload and wellbeing along with the opportunities it may present, before finally exploring low-cost ways to improve your professional practice through CPD and networking.

Subject knowledge

I'm certain every teacher recognises the importance of subject knowledge but finding time to improve it can be the biggest barrier. In this chapter, we will explore the importance of subject knowledge, how to we can go about developing our own and ways of keeping up to date with subject developments.

The importance of subject knowledge

Think about this for a moment; which is more important, knowing what you're teaching or knowing how to teach it? Throughout my career to-date this has been a contentious question. I'm not going to get into the arguments behind it, but I feel it is an important question to have you consider.

As a teacher, knowing and understanding the subject content allows for effective lesson planning and delivery. Subject knowledge allows for identification of common misconceptions and the effective planning and explanation of complex or challenging material. The UK Teachers' standards state for QTS we must "Demonstrate good subject and curriculum knowledge" expressing the fundamental nature of subject knowledge. Whilst research shows that "the most effective teachers have deep knowledge of the subjects they teach" (Coe et al., 2014), and without it learning is impeded.

Teachers' Standard 3

"Demonstrate good subject and curriculum knowledge".

- *Have a secure knowledge of the relevant subject(s) and curriculum areas, foster and maintain pupils' interest in the subject, and address misunderstandings.*

- *Demonstrate a critical understanding of developments in the subject and curriculum areas, and promote the value of scholarship.*

> • *Demonstrate an understanding of and take responsibility for promoting high standards of literacy, articulacy and the correct use of standard English, whatever the teacher's specialist subject.*
>
> Standards for Teaching: Subject knowledge, Department for Education, 2011

As a geographer, I've been quite lucky when it comes to developing subject knowledge. On a daily basis the news is full of relevant articles that take little time to read. I then tend to read the heavier content in the holidays to give me time to fully process and to reflect on the contribution it will make to my classroom practice.

However, whilst I taught history it was a different story and honestly much harder to fit in developing subject knowledge around lesson planning. I'd find myself reading one article, chapter or book that would lead onto having to read up on something else that would then lead to further reading around the subject to ensure I understood the full range of events, which ultimately led to the one I'd be teaching. I'm aware that even history specialists end up doing this; I always question how they have the time. Luckily for those I've discussed it with explain that for them it's more like reading for pleasure. But do we all have this luxury?

As educators how do we find the time to fit academic reading to enhance our subject knowledge into our already busy schedules?

Try this . . .

1   Have a clear understanding or outline of what knowledge you want to gain or enhance.

2   Take just twenty–thirty minutes a day or every few days to read subject specific material.

3   Write brief notes from your reading.

I've recently started to use Connell's note-taking strategy for my professional development reading with some minor adjustments.

I use the note column in the same way, writing down anything worthy of remembering. The cues column is used for writing down questions I could ask students whilst the summary section I note down how the reading relates to what I want or need my students to know, helping to identify the value to my classroom practice.

Personally, I find this strategy helpful in relating what I'm reading is relevant to what I'm teaching and how I can use it later on. I have a terrible habit however of forgetting to return to my note book when lesson planning and using the questions I've previously created. However, I do believe that by considering these as I read, it benefits teaching at a later date.

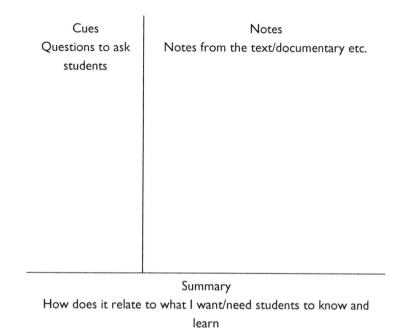

Cues Questions to ask students	Notes Notes from the text/documentary etc.

Summary
How does it relate to what I want/need students to know and
learn

Figure 11.1 Outline of how Cornell's note-taking strategy is used when developing subject knowledge

Strategies for developing knowledge

1 Identify needs and priorities

Before setting out researching and reading, ensure you know where your knowledge needs lie. Clarify what you will be teaching; that can be through the schemes of work, the curriculum and/or the exam specifications. Self-assess your understanding and prioritise the elements you have the least confidence in. Personally, I find RAG rating useful and employ the same technique with Key Stage 4 & 5 to aid students in identifying their revision priorities.

Next set out your priorities. If you're teaching something next week but have only highlighted it as amber, this is of greater priority than something you've rated red but won't teach until the end of the school year. Ensure you know the order of teaching as well as the content to be taught. Prioritise your learning.

Here's an example how Bethan White identified her subject knowledge needs during her NQT year.

2 Make use of subject experts

Subject experts can be found both in and out of schools and can provide a wealth of knowledge to enhance your subject understanding.

Subject Area	Sept 2017			Jan 2018			May 2018			Evidence
	R	A	G	R	A	G	R	A	G	
KEY STAGE 4										
The People's Health c. 1260 to present: Unit 1										Byrom, J & Riley, M (2016) The People's Health c. 1260 to present. Hodder Education: London. Lessons Taught: 11–09–17: Introduction and Course Overview 12–09–17: Did anyone really care about health in Mediaeval England? 18–09–17: Did anyone really care about health in Mediaeval England? 20–09–17: What were Mediaeval Responses to the Black Death? 02–10–17: What was public health like in towns and cities? 27–09–17: How did Public Health change in towns and cities?
The People's Health c. 1260 to present: Unit 2										Byrom, J & Riley, M (2016) The People's Health c. 1260 to present. Hodder Education: London. Lessons Taught: 03–10–17: Early Modern England 10–10–17: How did living conditions in the early modern period change? 13–10–17: How did living conditions in the early modern period change? 19–10–17: The Great Plague of 1665 28–10–17: Impact of Local governments 01–11–17: The Gin Craze 06–11–17: Summary of Unit – how much progress?

Subject Area	Sept 2017	Jan 2018	May 2018	Evidence
The People's Health c. 1260 to present: Unit 3				Byrom, J & Riley, M (2016) *The People's Health c. 1260 to present*. Hodder Education: London. Lessons Taught: 08–11–17: Overview of public health 1750–1900 17–11–17: Housing, food, water and waste in Industrial Britain 19–11–17: Housing, food, water and waste in Industrial Britain 21–11–17: What was the early Industrial Response to public health? 22–11–17: Why did people's attempts to stop the spread of plague in the period 1500–1750 have limited impact? EXAM Prep 23–11–17: The Great Stink of 1858
The People's Health c. 1260 to present: Unit 4				Byrom, J & Riley, M (2016) *The People's Health c. 1260 to present*. Hodder Education: London. Lessons Taught: 1–12–17: Do the changes in public health since 1900 tell a simple story of progress? 5–12–17: Public Health in the 20th C 13–12–17: C20th Gov involvement in smoking 18–12–17: What killed over 15 million people in 1918? 20–12–17: HIV and AIDS

Figure 11.2 An example of how to assess understanding of content to be taught from Bethan White

Within your school context, seek support from experienced or expert members of staff. Colleagues may well have had careers elsewhere before teaching. It's worth considering what expertise they can share with you and other staff. If your school or department doesn't already have a subject knowledge mentor programme, consider instigating the idea or setting one up yourself.

In setting up a subject knowledge mentor programme, staff identify subject content they are most confident with and sign up to be the 'topic expert'. These experts can then be the go to person for support, guidance and ideas for further reading. If your school is part of a MAT, it may be worth considering whether there are staff in the other schools that you can liaise with to develop your subject knowledge or to develop a mentor programme with.

Outside of your school context, you may wish to seek out subject experts in the field. I've found that Twitter has been fantastic for following academics from universities across the country for subject specific learning as well as pedagogy. Many are willing to answer questions, recommend reading and engage with teachers and students. If you're not a Twitter user, reach out through more traditional routes of communication such as email or phone; often you can find details of lecturers and academic staff on university websites.

If you happen to have connections in industry, use them as well. Whilst they may not be able to support you in terms of pedagogical practice associated with your specific subject, they can be helpful in highlighting new developments in the subject area, research and resources.

3 Subject associations

Subject associations are generally membership organisations that are independent of government and strive to support teachers in their subject specialism making them a useful source and wealthy source of knowledge. They can be a vast source of subject experts, and although you may not be able to speak to them one-to-one, many of the subject experts produce a variety of resources to support teacher subject knowledge and subject specific pedagogical practice.

Often subject associations are seen to be aimed at secondary and FE teachers specialising in a subject. Many associations also produce journals, resources and run CPD to develop their subject specific curriculum in primary schools and early years settings.

4 Subject snippets

Something I've seen in other departments but am yet to implement in my own is the concept of snippets of subject-specific CPD. There are a variety of approaches that can be taken with this delivery approach, but the main aim is to make it short and snappy, enhance subject knowledge without the burden of time. Five to ten

Subject Associations in the UK

National Association for the Teaching of English – www.nate.org.uk/

The English Association – https://www2.le.ac.uk/offices/english-association

Association of Teachers of Mathematics – www.atm.org.uk/

The Mathematical Association – www.m-a.org.uk/

Association for Science Education – www.ase.org.uk/

Geographical Association – www.geography.org.uk/

The historical association – www.history.org.uk/

Association of Physical Education – www.afpe.org.uk/

Design & technology association – www.data.org.uk/

Association for citizenship teaching – www.teachingcitizenship.org.uk/

National Association of Teachers of Religious Studies – www.natre.org.uk

Association for Language Learning – www.all-languages.org.uk/

The Association for Information Technology in Teacher Education – www.itte.org.uk/

The Incorporated Society of Musicians – www.ism.org/

Figure 11.3 List of Subject Associations in the UK

minutes should be sufficient to do justice. Share, discuss, reflect and takeaway. The following are three possible ways to implement this strategy.

Mini-subject sessions

Each member of staff takes it in turns to present one snappy session on a topic of interest. Several sessions can be run over a time frame such as over one hour or one per staff meeting. Whilst useful to engage staff in developing subject knowledge it may not necessarily be what you want when you need it. Therefore, it might be useful to consider a delivery calendar to correlate with the current content or medium-term planning.

Bring and share

A member of staff brings along an article from a journal, the news or the like. All staff read it, discuss it and consider its application to subject teaching.

Newsletter

Each member of the team submits a short summary of reading, news, research or similar to a collaborative newsletter. This can easily be done with an online platform such as Microsoft 360 or Google Drive. When complete share with the team.

5 Journals

Most subject associations produce their own journals, but the content may not always be what you are looking for at the time. I've found that it is only in recent years that I made use of academic journals when I want to develop my subject knowledge. I fell out of touch with using them after university and only rediscovered their effectiveness since taking on Key Stage 5 classes.

If you are lucky enough your school library may subscribe with one or more journal publishers. Check with your school librarian to find out if yours does; it may not be common knowledge.

Generally, I use Google Scholar to search for what I am looking for. Although many journals require a fee, there are also numerous ones that can be accessed for free in full or partially accessed. Usually I can find what I'm looking for in what's available and can use them as springboard to further research.

6 Books

Good old books. There is nothing like holding a solid book in your hands. I must admit I have plenty of books on teaching and learning, but so few subject specific books. I rarely invest in them unless they are a charm found on the dusty shelves of a charity shop. My husband on the other hand, he's a historian and he can't enough; books on whatever topic has him interested at any given moment. Books however can be a fantastic source of subject knowledge, even if academic books can be a bit on the pricey side.

If your department or primary school doesn't already have one, suggest setting up a shared book shelf or a book club of sorts. Encourage staff to bring in subject specific books for sharing.

7 Lectures and talks

Whilst you may not gain the knowledge you want in a time relevant fashion, lectures and talks are a fantastic source for widening your subject knowledge. Keep an eye on subject association websites for upcoming events, as well as the local newspapers, venues and organisations.

I've found that my local branch of Friends of the Earth put on a number of excellent talks by authors and climate scientists, whilst my local concert venue regularly has speakers. This year alone on they have had an audience with Dan Snow, Neil Oliver and Simon Reeve. Such events can be enlightening, educational and entertaining.

8 Social media

Love it or hate it, social media is huge source of inspiration. I find an incredible amount of material to develop my subject knowledge. At first, I didn't even realise how it was benefiting my classroom practice; now I can recognise when I refer to things I have read and try to keep an online collection of them. Much of what I find I probably would never have discovered if it weren't for Twitter and Facebook.

I highly recommend keeping an online collection of your digital reads for future reference. Websites and apps such as Flipboard and Pinterest are useful ways to collate articles and bookmark webpages in one place and allow access over a variety of devices. I also keep Flipboard collections for each exam board I teach and provide a link for my Key Stage 4 and 5 students to encourage further reading.

What about when you simply do not know the answer?

Teaching subjects outside of my academic realm led to many a learning opportunity. It's vital our students recognise that we are all learners; in fact, lifelong learners. Nobody will ever know everything there is to know. We should make the most of that and model learning practices for our students particularly in the age of knowledge at your fingertips.

When you don't know the answer, there are several approaches to take.

1   Pose the question back to the student and encourage them to think about it for a few minutes. Go away, find the answer, return to the student and ask them what they think. Discuss the answer with them.

2   Pose the question back to the student, ask them to discuss it with their peers to work out what they think the answer might be. Then do as with option 1.

3   Be honest. Tell the students you are unsure, but you'll find out together if you feel it's relevant to their learning and progress. Search for the answer on the internet using a reputable search engine and project it onto the whiteboard. I'd recommend ensuring you have safety lock on to ensure no unsuitable searches arise. Look through several sources of information with the students, ask them about the reliability of source, how does it compare to the previous, can it be trusted etc.

4   Respond with "good question, however we don't have time for that now". Propose the challenge to the student to find the answer out on their own accord and reward their additional learning. If they remember to find the answer, ensure their findings are shared with the class to make it worthwhile and to also allow you to deal with any misconceptions. If you pose such a challenge ensure you find out the answer as well, just in case they forget and to ensure the answer they find is accurate.

Takeaways

- Subject knowledge is essential for effective teaching.

- Assess your subject knowledge in line with what you will be teaching.

- Prioritise your subject knowledge development.

- Read little and often.

- Make the most of subject experts.

- It's okay to not know the answer to every question.

- Show students you never stop learning.

Reference

Coe, R., Aloisi, C., & Higgins, S. (2014) *What makes great teaching? Review of the underpinning research: Sutton trust* [Pdf] Available at www.suttontrust.com/wp-content/uploads/2014/10/What-Makes-Great-Teaching-REPORT.pdf

12 Progression

I never planned on becoming a middle leader, but I really wanted to work at my second school. It had the ethos and ideals I had been looking for in a school plus it was being set up by an organisation I held in high esteem. Whilst the school didn't exactly meet expectations, and I resented it in some respects, I did come away with a wealth of newly gained knowledge, experience and desires.

When I started in the role, during my second year of teaching, I was eager, hardworking and had the inability to say no. I was new enough to the profession to be easy to mould but with just enough classroom practice to be confident to take on the challenge. Additionally, I was a mightily naïve, people pleaser, happy to work my socks off to set up the department. The two years there were the hardest years of my life, and even though they broke me, what I took away was worth it.

My biggest takeaway was that I have strength, commitment and passion. I didn't know how much of these qualities I had until I was brave enough to admit my undoing, to apply for another teaching job, to decide to stay in the profession. The position taught me a great deal about myself, but this chapter isn't about the personal takeaways of taking on responsibility even though there are many.

Professionally speaking, the biggest takeaways from my first middle leadership position was the knowledge and understanding of curriculum development, assessment formation and provision of feedback. Without that first role as subject leader it would have taken me significantly longer to understand these elements.

Then there was working with other members of staff, in my case non-specialists, and learning to effectively disseminate good practice, to develop and put into practice a vision, creating tracking and monitoring systems, assessing and analysing subject-wide progress, the observation and improvement process, the list goes on. Whilst it was hard, the actual practice taught me more than reading books, blogs and journals would have ever done. It was the application that made the difference.

This chapter now looks at why responsibility is desirable, the debate on whether new teachers should take on responsibility during the formative years and the benefits and potential challenges of doing so.

Why take on responsibility?

We all have our reasons for taking on more responsibility either within our role or by changing roles, whether it be our own ambitions to move up the career ladder, a desire for a change in direction, the additional money or something else entirely. For most I imagine there is a sense of accomplishment and fulfilment in progression. As positive as that is, it can also be detrimental to the development of good and great teachers in the long term.

> ### Opportunity to think
>
> Where do you envisage yourself in five, ten or fifteen years from now?
> Is it money or aspiration that drives you?
> Can you take on responsibility and continue to develop your practice effectively?

The debate

There's a lot of debate surrounding early-career stage teachers taking on additional responsibility within their formative years of teaching. When I finished my PGCE in 2011, it was common place that at the end of the training that you'd complete a Career Entry Profile. This required newly qualified teachers to reflect on their strengths, areas for development and our aspirations. We were encouraged to consider the responsibility we would want to take on in the coming years and how we wanted out career to develop. I was already being asked to consider what I wanted to do beyond the day-to-day teaching.

What I understand now is that the first few years of teaching are the most important years for developing pedagogical practice. Yet with budget cuts along with recruitment and retention issues, more and more early-career teachers are asked or encouraged to step into roles of responsibility early on.

It may be desirable for schools to encourage good teachers through the ranks to leadership; the idea that if you are good in the classroom then you'll be good at leading a department or even leading whole school change. It may also be your desire and ambition to move to leadership quickly. But should we be propelling good teachers up the career ladder before they've truly mastered the art of teaching? Does this really help the school, the teacher or the retention crisis?

In May 2018, the UK's Government report 'School leadership in England 2010 to 2016: characteristics and trends' revealed that "more than three in ten school leaders that took up their posts between 2011 and 2015 had not been retained" (Department for Education, 2018). These figures were as high as "one in three" for secondary schools. As a result, schools have become increasingly keen to move new teachers into leadership roles to fill the gaps. School leaders are increasingly becoming younger and less experienced evident by 50% of new leaders in primary schools in 2016, having been qualified for nine years or less, whilst in secondary schools again 50% having only been qualified for seven years or less before taking on leadership roles, with promotion in London occurring within less than five years more likely.

Rather than propelling good teachers up the ranks with little experience, schools need to invest in professional development of teachers that show future leadership potential. They need to invest in support, training and a culture of development to help good teachers develop their practice first and foremost. They need and steady development of leaders instead of making it rushed and limited.

Should you take on responsibility early on in your career?

The benefits and challenges one may face when taking on further responsibility in the early stages of teaching will vary with context, role, your personal circumstances and experience as well as the support available.

Benefits may include your professional development, learning new skills, developing new relationships and deepening your understanding of school life. Whilst on the other hand it can increase your workload, impact your stress levels and worsen your work-life balance.

I took on a middle leadership role in just my second year of teaching. Was it a mistake? Possibly. Truthfully, I wasn't ready, I still had a lot to learn about general classroom practice, but I feel if I'd had the right support and coaching I may have found it less of a challenge. I often felt 'left to it' yet also felt under a great deal of pressure to perform as if I had prior experience of the position. Sometimes I feel that I should have remained as a classroom teacher for several more years before taking on responsibility to master and refine my practice. Other times I am highly appreciative of my experiences, despite being incredibly negative at times; taking on responsibility taught me a lot.

It's important to weigh up the impact additional responsibility may have on you, your workload and your career.

If you're considering taking on responsibility, consider the following:

- Is it something you've aspired to do or is it just happenstance?

- If it's something you've aspired to do? Is it likely to come up again in due course?

- Will you be provided with directed time to complete the associated tasks?

- Will the opportunity be of benefit to future aspirations?

- Will it be of benefit to your day-to-day classroom practice?

- Will it increase your workload or stress levels?

If after considering the above you still feel the role and responsibility is right for you, don't be afraid to speak to those that already undertake it and seek their advice and experiences before making your final decision.

Snippets of insight

I asked eduTwitter colleagues about their experiences of taking on responsibility and whether early-career teachers should do so. Here's what they had to say:

"I think you need to feel ready to take on responsibility, but this feeling of readiness depends on you, the responsibility, the support offered and other factors. There is rarely a right time for anything in this world! Think about where you want your career to go, what skill sets you need for the role, what others say about the job. There really is no such thing as bad experience". *Ed Brodhurst, Assistant Heateacher. Tweets as @brodhurst*

"I became Head of Geography in my sixth year of teaching. It allowed me to shape the nature of geography teaching at my school, including introducing a new field trip and helping the three new members of staff under me to develop their teaching. My advice would be only take on a responsibility if it something that you really feel capable of doing and are passionate about. Discuss your thoughts with others such as your line manager or those who have already taken responsibilities to see what the role will involve and whether it is manageable. In addition, consider how it might affect your personal relationships – will the new role significantly increase your workload?" *Sarah Larsen, Teacher of Geography. Tweets as @sarahlarsen74*

"I am troubled when NQTs find themselves as subject leaders or HoD by default; I think there is merit in taking a couple of years to 'arrive' as a teacher. However, some people are ready to assume responsibility earlier, for example, if an NQT had previously been an HLTA they might be ready after a year, other colleagues may need longer. It needs to be a combination of personal choice and mentoring/guidance from a trusted colleague or friend. I am worried by how quickly some people seem to arrive at senior leadership, because I think experience matters!" *Gill Rowland, Senior Lecturer at Canterbury Christ Church University. Tweets as @gillrowland1*

I've heard that a teacher should be considered a novice for the first ten years of their career. Many teachers find this very uncomfortable to hear, myself included. After a few years in the classroom I felt I had a good amount of expertise and experience. My teaching improved rapidly during and after my NQT year and I quickly became confident and self-assured. I became Key Stage 5 Coordinator three years into my career which helped me improve my subject knowledge quickly. After five, years I moved schools and was surprised to find I felt a bit like a NQT again. Different students and new challenges moved me out of my comfort zone, and suddenly I had a lot to learn. Then when I took of Head of Maths, eight years in I found I had little time for lesson planning. The most important part of my job – the teaching – became low priority. My teaching stagnated during that time. Over the years that followed I developed new skills and changed a lot of my approaches and routines. Ten years into my career I now am questioning everything. I have more expertise in teaching than ever before, but only now am reflective and mature enough to realise that I will always have a lot to learn as a teacher. Ten years of experience no longer feels like a lot. It takes time to realise that. *Jo Morgan, Maths Lead Practitioner, Harris Federation and UK Blog Award Winner 2017. Tweets as @mathsjem*

"I think the first few years should be spent really trying to become the best teacher you can be. Focus on that as, from experience, added responsibility detracts from everyday teaching. Early on I took on responsibility and whilst you get to influence how your school, or certain elements of it, are run; you don't get the time to do more work". *Adrian Bethune, Teacher and author of 'Wellbeing in the Primary Classroom: A Practical Guide to Teaching Happiness'. Tweets as @AdrianBethune*

"There is so many different aspects to becoming a good teacher. If you read widely and seek advice, then it takes at least five years to get to fulfil your potential in the classroom. Taking on additional responsibility in the first five years will mean sacrificing a fair amount of time that could be used refining your practice". *Rufus Johnstone, Lead Coach. Tweets as @rufuswilliam*

Takeaways

- Don't rush up the leadership ladder, take time to develop.

- Make the most of the first five years to hone your classroom practice.

- Don't be pressured into believing that to be a good teacher you have to take on responsibility.

- If the time is right and you feel ready for the next step, take it.

Reference

Department for Education (2018) *School leadership in England 2010 to 2016: Characteristics and trends* [Pdf] Available at www.gov.uk/government/publications/school-leadership-2010-to-2016-characteristics-and-trends [Accessed 18th August 2018]

13 CPD

In recent years, I've found myself fortunate enough to be able to go to quite a few conferences and education events, usually as a speaker. Yet I also get to go to sessions in the same way as any other attendee. If I'm honest it's the teacher-to-teacher events that have had the most impact on my practice; there's so much to learn from others. And when others talk with abundant passion and demonstrate a keenness to share their experiences, resources and ideas; how can you not go away feeling invigorated to teach and try new things? I'd go as far as to say teacher-to-teacher CPD events are my favourite kind of professional development; they combine pedagogical learning along with social activities, networking and the occasional bit of sightseeing.

Unfortunately, not everybody has the time or finances to be able to go to such events frequently. Many teachers rely on in-school training or local opportunities for professional development. Without personal sacrifices, such as using weekends, organising it yourself or spending your own money, it's become rarer for teachers to experience out of school professional development.

The importance of CPD

Continued professional development sounds incredibly impersonal, yet we each have our own needs and wants when it comes to developing our practice, knowledge and skills. Yet CPD provision is often variable, and all too often a one-size-fits-all approach is taken; so instead of calling it CPD, I think we should think of it more as personal professional development (PPD).

Planning for CPD

Start planning your professional development by assessing your current strengths, areas for improvement and your medium to long-term aspirations. Use this information to consider your PD goals for the academic year and beyond. Think

Professional Development Action Plan

Date: ___/___/___

Current Situation	
Personal Strengths	Areas for Development
Aims to achieve	Next Steps • • • • • • • •

Figure 13.1 Example of CPD action plan template

about what you want to achieve from your PD, what you need to do to achieve it and what you will do to turn it from aspiration to reality. Follow this by creating an action plan to help you achieve your PD goals.

Choosing the right CPD

With dwindling budgets and pressure on resources, choosing the right CPD is indispensable. A positive session or event that inspires your practice, gives you plenty to takeaway and gets your mind buzzing can be just what is needed to invigorate you and your practice. On the other hand, a session or event that leaves you feeling drained, resentful and wondering about the purpose simply leaves you negative and insipid by the experience. Good CPD doesn't have to involve a day off timetable; it doesn't have to involve large costs and doesn't have to be prescribed. There are a wide variety of ways to access low-cost CPD which are outline below.

With your CPD goals in mind, you may wish to seek courses that meet your needs. I recommend browsing www.cpdforteachers.com for inspiration and list of courses across the UK.

Low-cost CPD

1 Read

One of the cheapest forms of CPD I've discovered has to be reading – whether it be blogs, education magazines or books. It can be relevant, timely and completed in snippets. I've often experienced that internal CPD has rarely been relevant and timely for my development needs. For instance, the example that stands out in my mind was during my NQT year. We didn't have a twilight session on behaviour management until around February, yet behaviour was probably one of the most influential factors that affected our teaching. Instead of waiting until the CPD session I took action and did my own research and reading. I found Sue Cowley's 'Getting the Buggers to Behave' noteworthy. Whilst in the classroom I tried and tested a variety of techniques in an attempt to discover what worked best for me and my students.

Personally, I find reading an inspiring process; my head fills with ideas that I want to try in my classroom, and although I may not agree with everything I read, reading provides time for reflection and development.

2 TeachMeets

I've found TeachMeets to be an invaluable opportunity for free CPD. There are a wide variety taking place around the UK and other countries. A TeachMeet is a rather informal event for teachers to share good practice, ideas and pedagogy. Generally speaking, participants present takeaway ideas in bitesize snippets for the audience on a general theme or topic; some events have key note speakers that speak on a topic or issue for longer, and there are some take a workshop approach.

TeachMeets can cover a range of themes, topics or issues, many focusing on general teaching and learning such as TMEnfield, whilst learning such as TMHistoryIcons and TMGeographyIcons are more subject specific. On the rise are TeachMeets that focus on wellbeing, workload and mental health.

In addition to TeachMeets there are many free or low-cost conferences being held on Saturday's. Conferences such as Pedgoo Hampshire, Northern Rocks and the Teaching and Learning Takeover have had a big influence on my classroom practice. Whilst attending such events may seem like an additional loss of time to the job, I personally feel the benefits, and I'm sure many will agree outweigh this. Each event I've attended has made me feel empowered, inspired and enthused to get back into the classroom on Monday. They've helped to reignite my fire time and time again, whilst allowing me to meet some incredible people.

Pete Sanderson (Tweets as @LessonToolbox) maintains a useful education conference calendar for events in the UK which can be found at http://lessontoolbox. wordpress.com/edu-conference-national-calendar/

3 EduTwitter

EduTwitter is an incredible source of information for educators. I know I wouldn't be in teaching any more if I hadn't joined Twitter in September 2014. At first, I made use of Twitter merely to share some of my ideas and resources; now it's an empowering tool that I has helped to keep me in teaching. If I hadn't discovered #Teacher5aday and my personal learning network that has developed through interactions with others, my days in teaching would have ended a long time ago. Twitter has been the source of much inspiration. If you need a resource, someone will have something. If you need advice, someone would have been through similar. If you need to talk, someone will listen. Ideas are shared freely, advice is given openly, and support is given widely. Whatever you are looking for to help you to develop professionally there will be something there for you.

4 Online courses

The internet provides invaluable opportunities for further learning. With sites from educational institutes such as the Open University who own Future Learn and Tes, there are a wide range of free or low-cost courses out there. Additionally, subject associations, charities and other organisations may offer online courses to suit your needs.

Useful Links

www.futurelearn.com
www.open.edu/openlearn
www.tes.com/institute/cpd-courses-teachers
www.udemy.com
www.teachertoolkit.co.uk/online-training
www.rogershistory.com/cpd
http://chartered.college/chartered-college-events
http://education.microsoft.com
http://teachercenter.withgoogle.com/

5 Subject associations

Subject associations provide a variety of opportunities from journals and books to online and face-to-face courses. Additionally, you'll find events, lectures, new updates and teaching resources to support and develop your practice.

6 Drop in T&L sessions

Depending of the size of the department or staff body running several sessions at a time to share a piece of subject knowledge may be doable. Several staff share, and several staff attend.

7 PD book club

A teaching and learning book club can bring staff together in an informal but developmental way. Choose a book, a chapter, a journal, a blog or similar to read over a set period. Once everyone has had the opportunity to read the selected reading, find time to meet and discuss. This could be over a working lunch, during a department meeting or during other directed time. Wouldn't it be great if all schools gave over some directed time to professional reading and discussion? I digress.

The reading maybe associated with a specific technique or subject content or wider such as a pedagogical theory, strategy or idea.

8 TED talks and podcasts

Whether you're looking to develop subject knowledge or pedagogical understanding there is a TED talk or podcast out there somewhere to meet your needs. I love how technology has enabled twenty-four-hour access to information. I like to listen to them as I walk home from work. I know others that listen whilst driving. It's a great use of that time.

Engage with research

It may seem daunting and time consuming but engaging with research is a powerful tool to develop your classroom practice. There are a wide variety of sources available from blogs to academic journals freely available. Whilst I did plenty of reading during my PGCE year, I'd forgotten a lot of it by the time by NQT year came around. I didn't start to engage with research again until I started setting up a department. A lot of what I read influenced my planning and curriculum development. Nowadays I use research to develop my practice and that of others. Research can be as simple as reading up, implementing and reflecting or more in depth such as implementing a trial or strategy and measuring the impact.

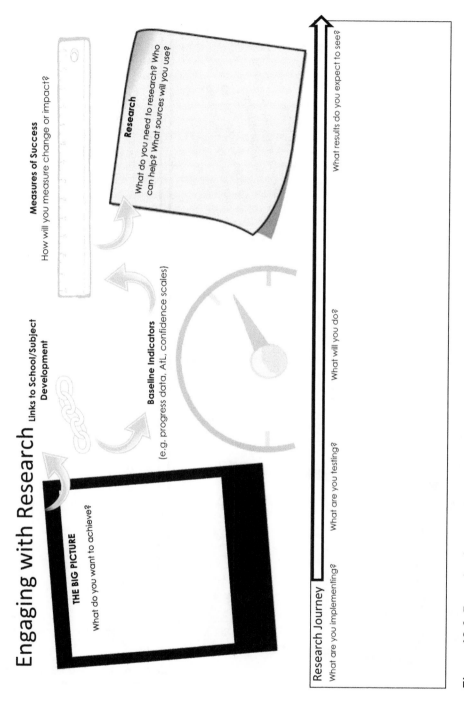

Figure 13.2 Example of action plan template to help teachers engage with research

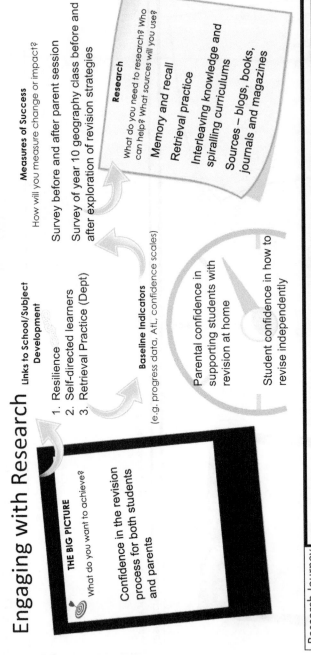

Figure 13.3 Example of completed action plan

This year I'm exploring effective retrieval strategies to help my students to develop techniques to recall and revise content. I've identified effective strategies and will be explicitly teaching several of them to my GCSE students. In addition, I'll be working with a colleague to deliver 'How to Revise' sessions to parents and carers. To develop this, I created a planning sheet to bring my research ideas together. I found this really useful, and it's now been shared across the school to help our staff engage with research as part of the professional development programme.

Opportunity to think

If you're unsure where to start with research, consider the following questions:

What do you want to achieve with your research?

How will it improve your classroom practice?

What links does it have to whole school or subject development?

What bassline indicators will you explore?

What will you measure to determine success or impact?

What theories underpin or support what you want to achieve?

Who can support you in your research?

Snippets of insight

I posed the question "What advice would you give new teachers in regard to CPD??" to eduTwitter colleagues. Here's what they had to say:

"Link your CPD activities to a wider goal – think about where you want your career to go, set some targets and devise activities that help you get there. I wanted to develop my career as a teacher of outdoor learning and to get there, I convinced my school to pay for my Mountain Leader award, and it took me to Nepal, India and Morocco, additionally I now run the school climbing wall. A good SLT will listen to ideas they haven't thought of which help develop student experiences". *Ed Brodhurst, Assistant Headteacher. Tweets as @brodhurst*

"Be proactive about identifying your needs and seeking out ways of meeting them – ownership is important! Broaden your horizons as to what constitutes CPD. Networking, TeachMeets and reading all count". *Gill Rowland, Senior Lecturer at Canterbury Christ Church University. Tweets as @gillrowland1*

"Join Twitter or local networks. Talk about teaching. Read books about teaching. Chat with colleagues about lessons. Know that you will always have a lot more to learn. Teaching is a science and needs to be studied. And no matter how relevant your degree was, your subject knowledge can always be better". *Jo Morgan, Maths Lead Practitioner, Harris Federation and UK Blog Award Winner 2017. Tweets as @mathsjem*

"Soak up as much as you can! Go on courses, read books and learn your craft. If you go on a course, make the time to reflect and look at how to embed what you've learnt". *Adrian Bethune, Teacher and author of 'Wellbeing in the Primary Classroom – A Practical Guide to Teaching Happiness'. Tweets as @AdrianBethune*

Takeaways

- Make your professional development personal.

- CPD is more than just INSET days, broaden what constitutes as CPD.

- Use your time wisely, short snippets can be as effective as whole days.

- CPD can be free and low cost.

- Have a vision and aim for your professional development.

- Engage with research where possible.

14 Networking

Teaching can be a lonely career, despite being surround by people all day. It can feel like you're fighting alone in your classroom to get good results for your students. It can feel like you're the only one that has issues with a student. It can feel like you're missing out on events with family and friends because you have work that just must be done. It can feel like you're on your own. But you're not; that's important to remember.

Networking in whatever form you choose to partake is advantageous, not only for professional development but for feeling like you are part of something; a network of educators.

For me, networking with teachers outside of my school helped me to feel less lonely. I had been a lone geographer in charge of Humanities whilst also teaching GCSE IT. The team of other subject leaders were friendly, helpful and great at their jobs, but did we have any time to talk and collaborate? No!

Yet by using Twitter I was able to spend half an hour or so socialising with other educators without having to leave my house. I could ask for resources whilst I worked; I could seek out support when I needed it and ask for guidance when I was unsure, all of which I would have had to have waited to do if I wanted to do it with the people I worked with. It was almost instant.

As previously mentioned I've been fortunate enough to attend several face-to-face conferences and education events each year. This has enabled me to network both online and offline, increasing my reach to other great geographers, educators and academics from which to learn.

Networking online or offline

Personally, I enjoy a bit of both, but there is no doubt that networking offline is much harder, more time consuming and creates smaller connections than networking online.

To meet in person, you have to organise, plan and find time to meet. Whereas online it can be done in your home, on the train, during your lunch break, wherever. Nevertheless, offline networking is not impossible. Meet up with other subject specialists or educators in your area. If there's nothing already set up, consider creating a regular meet up. Advertise to local schools, make it free of charge, in or out of school.

Generally, I find offline networking goes hand-in-hand with online networking. Meet, exchange emails or Twitter handles (the latter more frequently) and keep in touch.

How to get started with networking online

First of all, decide what would work best for you, short and snappy through something like Twitter or Facebook or something that requires more investment like subject or teaching forums.

When I first started teaching, I found the SLN Geography Forum useful for subject specific matters and TES forums for general education. These I felt required investment of time, it wasn't exactly easy to search posts and threads could become quite long and tedious. When I discovered the Twitter education network in 2014, I figured I'd give it a go. For me it's been life changing. I could drop in and out as a when required. I could access it on the go and return to it at a time that suited me.

Next decide how much time you'll dedicate to networking. Don't let it take over your life. It can be very tempting to spend hours talking education outside of school. But you need that work-life balance. Will you dip in and out or set a dedicated time each day for 'educational networking'?

Lastly, choose a name that will represent you now and in the future. Try to avoid names that involve acronyms like NQT and RQT. You won't be newly or recently qualified forever; choose a username that will carry through year on year.

Personal learning networks

A personal or professional learning network (PLN) is a way of using social media and technology to connect, collaborate and communicate with colleagues (okay, more like educators from around the world, but I liked the alliteration there) to support ongoing learning and professional growth.

Yet, before social media, PLNs were nothing new. Naturally teachers and educators seek support and inspiration from others, whether in their own school or from schools locally. Although some would be more proactive in creating those connections than others; teachers have rarely worked in isolation. Technology has just made easier by removing the spatial and temporal barriers allowing more of us to connect, collaborate and share.

Why create a PLN?

The great thing about a PLN is that you can make it what you want it to be; you can choose who to follow and who to connect with. You can make your PLN as wide or as small as you wish; you can make it local or far reaching, you can make it join up with your thinking or challenge it, you can choose to follow or block. You have choice over how you use and connect with your network.

A PLN is for your professional development and your professional learning, so customise it. It's yours to control. Consider your aspirations, your opinions, your subject and create it around that.

But in case you need them, here are five reasons to create a PLN

1   It gives you control over your professional development.

   You no longer have to wait for the training to be provided; you can seek out what you need when you need it. Plus, there's the opportunity to explore content that interests you and not what somebody else thinks you need or should know. You can take charge and be in control.

2   There's advice, support and guidance when you need it.

   If you're struggling with an aspect of your teaching, subject content or maybe something more personal; help is at hand. All you need to do is say something. Generally, educators are willing to share ideas, support and resources. You can ask directly or find threads on the matter of interest.

3   There's flexibility to where and when you participate.

   You have the freedom to choose when and where to access your PD. It's 24/7, but that doesn't mean you have to be online all the time. You can dip in and out as you please, invest in it as much or as little as you want. No more waiting for the training session to take place.

4   There's a lot of Variety.

   As well as there being the flexibility to choose when you engage, there's also the variety of how you engage. Through your PLN you can learn and connect in a way that suits you; many use Twitter and Facebook; others choose forums, podcasts and blogs. The potential PLN platforms are forever developing with technological change. Additionally, how you engage can vary; you may choose to engage in general education chat, join in the array of discussions and debates or merely observe from afar. It's your choice.

5   You'll be globally connected

   As a geographer, this one truly sparks my interest. The development of PLNs through social media means we are more globally connected than ever before meaning we can access a variety of opinions, ideas and resources from different contexts; we can stay current on research and best practice globally, nationally and even locally and can enrich our understanding of the world and education to better prepare our students for the global society in which they live. Developing a PLN means we open ourselves up to a world of experts, academics and professionals that provide multiple perspectives on education that can challenges our ideas and improve our practice. In addition, our global connectedness is positive modelling to our students on how to use technology and social media for good.

Getting started online

My reason for setting up the blog and joining Twitter had been my desire to discuss and share. In my first school, I shared all my resources with the rest of my department. We discussed pedagogy and our subject. When I moved to the second school, I led a department of one specialist, me. Others used my resources to teach their lessons, but that was more for consistency than anything else. We didn't discuss the learning, the purpose, the subject. Blogging and tweeting meant I could do that.

It also meant I could share the resources I spent time making to benefit others. Workloads were increasing, and I thought if my resources meant someone didn't have to make it, they could spend the time on more important things. One thing led to another and I now I have a huge PLN that influence my practice on a day to day basis.

So now you're convinced, where do you start?

Opportunity to think

Before you get started, determine your needs and goals.

- What do you want out of your PLN?

- Interested in sharing resources?

- Looking for inspiration?

- Want to join in with debate and discussion?

- Subject specific or general pedagogy?

    Knowing what you want out of a PLN will give you direction and somewhere to start.

Creating a PLN: setting up

First off, create your online presence. I'd suggest starting with Twitter. Set up an account and as previously mentioned remember to create a username that doesn't circumscribes to a particular time in your career. I'd recommend adding information to your profile based on your interests, mine for example goes something like this "Married to the job since 2012. Head of #geography & #IBESS #IBGeog19 #MYP #UKBA18 finalist #FeedbackNOTmarking #MagpiedPedagogy #teacher5adaybuddybox". The use of hashtags makes me findable and helps others to identify my interests.

Next, follow educators. They can be tricky to find at first. Start by following someone you know (you can find my tweets at @MrsHumanities) and see who they are following.

You can search for teachers on twitter by subject here: www.classtools.net/ twitter4teachers/.

Then I'd suggest searching for a term of interest by searching for hashtags such as #geographyteacher or #primaryteacher. This will provide you with people that have used these terms or hashtags either in tweets or in their profile.

Before following anyone, take a look at their recent tweets and consider the following

- Are they frequent users?

- How do they align to your educational ethos?

- Will they support or challenge your thinking?

- Do they share what you want out of your PLN?

If you're happy with your answers, follow them. If not, then don't feel obliged to follow them and move on. You will find that as you follow more people, your circle of contacts expands opening you up to more interesting ideas, conversations and people.

Once you're set up, you'll want to introduce yourself. Start by sending a tweet that outlines your interests and aims for your Twitter PLN. The following are a few examples to help get you started.

"New #tweacher, very excited to develop my #PLN. Interested in #SEND #coaching and #maths".

"First tweet, hoping to share ideas, resources and inspiration for #primary teachers".

If you're feeling shy, don't worry, you may just want to use it to access others tweets rather than engage in tweeting yourself until you are comfortable.

Creating a PLN: Twitter chats

Once you're set up and following people, you might fancy joining a Twitter chat. These are groups of educators that meet on Twitter at an agreed time, using an agreed hashtag to discuss an agreed topic of interest. Some are a one-hour weekly forum such as #NQTChat #GeogChat and #PrimaryRocks. Whilst others run for longer such as the #Teacher5aday #SlowChat which develops over a week, each day being led by someone new.

You can find a wide variety of global Twitter chats on this website https://sites. google.com/site/Twittereducationchats/home

The benefit of joining in with a Twitter chat is not only that they help to build your PLN with likeminded people, but they also provide an opportunity for educators to discuss topics of interest with people from a variety of contexts with a range of perspectives supporting the development of professional practice.

Tips for Twitter chats

1   It is okay to lurk. It is acceptable to follow the discussion rather than participate. You can join in if you want and whenever you are ready. Usually chats are supportive, so if you're a little scared, introduce yourself before starting and mention it's your first time. People will empathise.

2   Chats can move quickly. It can be hard to keep up with each and every response. Don't panic. You can return to the chat afterwards if you need to either by searching the hashtag, or if you're lucky the organiser might archive the chat. Don't feel you have to read everything that is said.

3   Remember to read the questions posed. Sometimes you might pick up a chat response part way through. Ensure you read the questions that form the chat to help you to understand the discussion. It's easy to misinterpret someone's response without the full picture.

There are plenty of tools and apps to help follow and engage in a Twitter chat such as Tweetdeck, Tweetchat or Twubs.

The following chats are correct as of November 2018.

How to create a Twitter chat

1   Create an account to host the chat.

2   Create the hashtag.

3   Set a day and time of the week/month.

4   Create an advert and share it to raise awareness of your chat.

5   Put a request out for hosts.

6   Set up a google form to collect details from potential hosts.

7   Put the hosts into a calendar to spread out the topics for discussion.

8   Inform your hosts of schedule.

9   Create an image for each of the questions to be asked or ask your hosts to do so.

Topic	Hashtag	Description	Twitter Account	Frequency
General Education	#behaviourchat	Forum to discuss behaviour & attendance issues within schools	@BehaviourChat	Weekly
	#CCTBookClub	Book discussion from the Chartered College of Teaching	@CharteredColl	Monthly
	#debatED	Weekly debate on all things educational	@ed_debate	Weekly
	#pedagoofriday	Community of teachers learning through sharing classroom practice	@pedagoo	Weekly
	#PlanningPanic	Discuss ideas, teaching tips and resources requests	@PlanningPanic	Weekly
	#SENexchange	A place to share news, ideas, resources & chat about issues related to SEND	@SENexchange	Weekly
	#TwinklTeach	Teacher-led education chat on a range of topics	@twinklresources	Weekly
	#UKFEchat	Community of and forum for Further Education professionals	@theukfechat	Weekly
	#UKEdChat	UK education chat on a wide range of topics.	@ukedchat	Weekly
	#UKEdResChat	Chat about education research – methods, ethics, impacts & more.	@UKEdResChat	Weekly
	#UKpastoralchat	Forum for discussion of pastoral matters	@UKpastoralchat	Monthly
New teachers	#ITTchat	A chat for anyone interested or partaking in Initial Teacher Training	@ITTchat	Weekly
	#NQTchat	Weekly chat for teachers from ITT to experienced professionals on the topic of NQTs	@NQTUK	Weekly
Leadership	#mltchat2	A forum for Middle Leaders to share ideas and support one another	@MLTChat2	Weekly
	#NewToSLTChat	Collaboration, reflection & support, for aspiring & new leaders.	@NewToSLT	Weekly
	#SLTchat	Discussion for all teachers interested in UK school leadership	@SLTchat	Weekly
	#UKGovChat	A place for UK school governors to share good practice, support & challenge each other	@UKGovChat	Weekly

Figure 14.1 Table of Twitter chats

Topic	Hashtag	Description	Twitter Account	Frequency
Primary Specific	#EYshare	Forum to share and discuss the Early Years	@EarlyYearsIdeas	Weekly
	#PrimaryRocks	Primary focused edchat	@PrimaryRocks1	Weekly
Subject Specific	#ASEchat	Chat for everything to do with science education from the Association for Science Education	@theASE	Weekly
	#caschat	Chat on Computing and Computer Science	@clcsimon	Weekly
	#EngChat	Chat for English Teachers by English Teachers	@EngChatUK	Weekly
	#ELTChat	Chat for English Language professional from around the world	@ELTchat	Weekly
	#GeogChat	Forum to discuss and debate topics and issues in geographical education.	@GeogChat	Weekly
	#HistoryChatUK	Forum to discuss all things history	@HistoryChatUK	Weekly
	#mathschat	Maths Chat	@BetterMaths	Weekly
	#mathscpdchat	Discussions on mathematics CPD from the National Centre for Excellence in the Teaching of Mathematics	@mathscpdchat	Weekly
	#REChatUK	RE based discussion and resource sharing		Monthly
	#STEMchat	A chat to bring together parents, educators + STEM professionals to share resources and ideas.	@STEMchat	Monthly
	#ukPEchat	Discuss and share ideas with other PE professionals	@ukPEchat	Monthly
Slow chat	**#Teacher5aday** **#SlowChat**	A slow chat focused on teacher wellbeing	**@teacher5aday**	During school holidays

Figure 14.1 (Continued)

10 Using TweetDeck schedule the tweets with the questions, images and hashtag.

11 Before each chat, change the password and share with the upcoming host.

12 The scheduled tweets will be published automatically at the time set. The host then prompts discussion, retweets participant responses, and if possible, they try to reply to participants leaving you to participate.

Creating a PLN: Facebook

Facebook is a useful tool for developing your PLN although slightly different to Twitter. It'll require you to join education groups or follow education-based pages.

The benefit of education-based pages is that you'll see updates on your timeline. There is generally little interaction from the wider education community and may appear as links and images. Whereas education groups involve the development of a community with a purpose. They are great for disseminating ideas, resources and links as well as discussing topics of interest.

There are now a wide range of education-based groups on Facebook, bringing together hundreds and in some cases thousands of educators with a shared interest. The 'AQA GCSE Geography Teachers Group' is a great example of this. Although not affiliated with the exam board, this group created by Rob Chambers and Andrew Boardman provides thousands of geography educators with access to shared resources, discussion and links to materials to support the development of the recently introduced GCSE course. It's not the only group of its kind, but it's one of the biggest I've come across.

The following table provides a range of Facebook groups. To find these groups simply go to Facebook and type the name in the search bar. This is far from an exhaustive list, more a taste of what can be found. For subject-specific groups simply search for your subject.

Creating a PLN: other media

From Twitter, you'll probably start to develop an awareness of other forms of media that will feed into your PLN such as blogs, podcasts and forums.

Using websites that enable you to bookmark or pin webpages such as Pinterest and Flipboard can be useful for keeping track of inspiration and reading.

You may even wish to branch out and create your own blog to share your thoughts and ideas. Blogging sites such as Wordpress and Blogger are free and easy to use.

Personally, I've found blogging a great way to develop my practice through reflection on what I do. I've been able to share resources and teaching ideas along with discussing issues that matter. Blogging isn't for everyone, but if you're interested maybe give it a try.

Topic	Name	Description
New teachers	Twinkl Trainee and Student Teachers Group	A group for support, ideas and inspiration for student teachers
	Twinkl NQT and RQT Group – Newly and Recently Qualified Teachers	A group for support, ideas and inspiration for new professional educational practitioners
Primary Specific	Primary Teachers	A group for primary teachers to share resources, ideas and attempt to relieve stress!
	Primary School Leaders	A professional group for all school leaders.
	Primary Teaching – NQT and Trainee teachers	Support group for those in training or NQT year
SEN	Twinkl SEN Educators Group	A group for support, ideas and inspiration for teachers and professional practitioners working in SEN settings
	Ideas and support for SENCOS/Teachers/TAs who work with SEN children	A chance to share views and ideas for anybody working with children who has special educational needs
	SENCo/SENDCo Support (Professionals)	A group for SENCo's and those that work within SEN settings to support, share ideas and to share good practice.
Wellbeing	Twinkl Teaching Well-Being Group	A welcoming and supportive group, for staff in schools to share ideas to aid a healthy lifestyle and wellbeing
	#Teacher5adayBuddyBox	An online community for participants to share ideas, photos and general wellbeing chatter

Figure 14.2 Table of Facebook groups

Takeaways

- Networking can be online or offline.
- Networking is a powerful tool for professional development.
- Twitter is an excellent source of information and inspiration.
- A PLN can be both a source of learning and support.
- Don't be afraid to reach out, join in or request help.

# Conclusion

My first five years of teaching were just a learning curve, a rollercoaster of emotions and a lesson in determination and resilience. I had many very, very low moments with depression, anxiety and stress impacting my health, friendships and wellbeing. But it was also a period that taught me a lot.

Conclusion

What has five years in teaching taught me?

The short answer is a hell of a lot.

I know how I teach now. I know my preferences. I know how to learn about learning. I know what I like in the classroom and what I don't. I know what makes for good practice for me, and I know what doesn't. I know how to be flexible but also how to be consistent. I know how to balance my work and my life. I know I've grown as a practitioner and will continue to do so.

But I only know all of this because I've tried so much and learnt so much. I've experienced good times and experienced bad times. I've had the opportunity to explore and try new things. I've taken the time to read and research, to talk and discuss, to share and to steal (ideas). Without all my prior experiences in how to deal with behaviour and being overburdened with workload from marking and feedback, assessment, data analysis, planning etc. I wouldn't have become the teacher I am today.

I honestly believe it takes finding the right school to really make you enjoy the job and love this all-important career. If you're not happy where you are, try a few places before making the big decision to leave teaching forever. You just have to find what's right for you.

When I came to the end of my fifth year in teaching, I was thankful that I'd remained as a statistic of survival. I'm staying in education because deep down, I love teaching those young humans who will one day be grown up humans that will make decisions about our world. I want them to make responsible ones that benefit and support each and every one of us, that respect their future colleagues and their kid's teachers, that look after their communities and wider environment, that abolish homelessness and poverty, that fight diseases and find cures and that innovate and design. I want them to be able to learn so that they create a better world than we have today. And that's why I'm staying in teaching.

From leaving to staying

I came close to leaving teaching in 2016. I had started writing applications for jobs outside of teaching because I hated the anxiety I woke with every day, the stress of the workload and the pressure of poor behaviour. Leaving teaching felt like the only option.

But an opportunity arose during the Easter break right before I went through my breakdown, I'd seen an advert for a job at a local grammar school. I didn't initially apply for it for two reasons: firstly, I didn't agree with a selective school system; secondly, I feared it would be more of the same. But I knew that if I didn't, I'd be handing in my notice that term and leaving teaching for good.

After much encouragement, I decided I would give teaching one more chance before I parted ways with the profession, and the application was submitted minutes before the deadline.

During my time off, I received the news that my application had been successful, and I was invited to interview. This put me into a conundrum; could I really go for an interview at another school whilst I was signed off sick?

I accepted the invite to interview but again it took a great deal of persuasion from my family.

I worried in the lead up to the interview day.
What if I don't look well enough?
What if they can tell if I'm currently emotionally unstable?
What if I've lost the ability to teach?
What if I burst into tears mid-interview?
What if this school is as bad as the last?
What if I don't even get the job, will I still stay in teaching?
What if, what if . . . so many what ifs went through my mind.

I remember being incredibly nervous on the day of interview, more so than usual. There were such an array of thoughts whirling around my head. I couldn't think straight but at least I knew my stuff, it was there somewhere. I just had to draw it out.

Thankfully, the team that observed and interviewed me could see past the nerves and anxiety I very obviously exerted. Shortly after leaving the school gates, the job was offered to me.

During the interview process I explained that despite being very pleased with the school, if I were to be offered the job I would need time to think about the decision. They were happy to give me that time to think and I could come back with my decision in due course.

The big decision

I struggled with the decision for the rest of the day.

I wanted to leave my current school, but I didn't want to leave all the work I'd put into developing the department from scratch. I didn't want to leave so many of the students I had come to know so well. I didn't want to leave some of my colleagues with which I'd formed friendships.

But then the decision was made for me when I contacted my employer, the current Headteacher. I explained the circumstances. I tried to explain my thoughts. The response however made me recognise my true value to that school. I was easily replaceable.

I then felt I had no commitment to stay.

That phone call made the decision for me. I later contacted the new school and accepted the offer. Whilst it was a challenging decision to make and many tears were shed, it has been a truly rewarding decision to try another school.

Do you stay or leave?

If you're struggling with micro-management or a toxic environment, don't feel it's your fault. The leadership culture has a lot to do with it. Don't think all schools are the same.

If you're considering leaving teaching, but if teaching is what you truly want to do, try another school or even two before you leave for good. It might well be the environment as opposed to the job.

Finding the right place can be tricky, some schools look great on paper, but you'll never really know how staff and wellbeing are supported until you visit the school or even begin working there. But there are ways to work out if it will be a good match for you.

Tips for finding a match

Once you've taken the decision to apply to other schools, it can be challenging to know what to look for. Here are my top tips

1   Look over the school policies, particularly those associated with assessment, reporting progress and feedback. How often do they assess students? How regularly do they report to parents on student progress? Do they have a required frequency for providing written feedback? Do they allow staff to decide the appropriate feedback methods?

2   Do they have a wellbeing policy or charter? Are teachers mentioned as well as students?

3   If possible, visit the school in advance. What kind of feel do you get from the school tour? Do staff appear happy? Do staff and students talk positively of the school experience? Do they let you speak to the member of staff you'd be replacing?

4   At interview ask how they support staff wellbeing. Consider the response carefully. Are you confident with it? Try not to be bowled over by 'wellbeing days' and other token gestures. Do they discuss managing workload? Do they mention ensuring a work-life balance for staff?

Going forward

As a profession, we have a lot to look forward to. There is change on the horizon. Awareness of stress, workload and impacts on mental health for staff in schools is on the rise. There are more and more of us that are standing up and making our voices heard. Not only that but there are more of us taking charge, sharing ideas and implementing change.

You have the power to influence no matter what stage you are in your career. If you're willing to fight and stand up for yourself and your profession there's no reason why you should become a statistic of resignation. Instead strive to be a statistic of success, determination and change. Together we can change the education system and improve our wellbeing, workload and work-life balance.

Takeaways

- Not all schools are the same, try others before deciding teaching isn't for you.

- Take charge of your wellbeing, be proactive and persistent.

- Change is happening in schools, be bold and be part of that change.

Index